England

England

By Jean F. Blashfield

Enchantment of the World™
Second Series

Children's Press®

An Imprint of Scholastic Inc.

New York Toronto London Auckland Sydney
Mexico City New Delhi Hong Kong
Danbury, Connecticut

Frontispiece: Guard at Buckingham Palace

Consultant: Laura Beers, Assistant Professor of History, American University, Washington, D.C.

Please note: All statistics are as up-to-date as possible at the time of publication.

Book production by The Design Lab

Library of Congress Cataloging-in-Publication Data
Blashfield, Jean F.
  England/by Jean F. Blashfield.
      p. cm.—(Enchantment of the world—second series)
  Includes bibliographical references and index.
  ISBN: 978-0-531-27542-9 (lib. bdg.)
  1. England—Juvenile literature. I. Title.
  DA27.5.B58 2012
  942—dc23   2012000503

1 2 3 4 5 6 7 8 9 10 R 22 21 20 19 18 17 16 15 14 13

England

Contents

Cover photo:
Royal wedding

CHAPTER

 ONE "This Precious Stone" 8

TWO Land and Sea 14

THREE Natural England 26

FOUR Through the Centuries 34

FIVE Monarchs and Ministers 58

SIX The World of Work 70

SEVEN People and Language 82

 EIGHT Spiritual Life 92

 NINE Art and Sports 100

 **TEN** Food and Fun 116

Lake District

Timeline **128**

Fast Facts **130**

To Find Out More **134**

Index **136**

Red fox

C H A P T E R

O N E

"This Precious Stone"

T HE OLDEST KNOWN NAME FOR ENGLAND IS ALBION. It appeared in writing as early as the sixth century BCE. In the twelfth century CE, an archbishop named Geoffrey of Monmouth wrote that thousands of years earlier, Albion had been inhabited only by a few giants. He went on to say that Albion was appealing because of "the pleasant situation of the places, the plenty of rivers abounding with fish, and the engaging prospect of its woods." For several centuries his description was accepted as accurate. The "pleasant situation" was certainly true, but Geoffrey's giants make him England's first science fiction writer.

Opposite: **Hundreds of rivers cut across the English landscape.**

What Is England?

England is the southern two-thirds of the island of Great Britain. The northern part of Great Britain is Scotland, and the western part is Wales. Neither England, Scotland, nor Wales is a separate nation today. Not even the entire island of Great Britain is

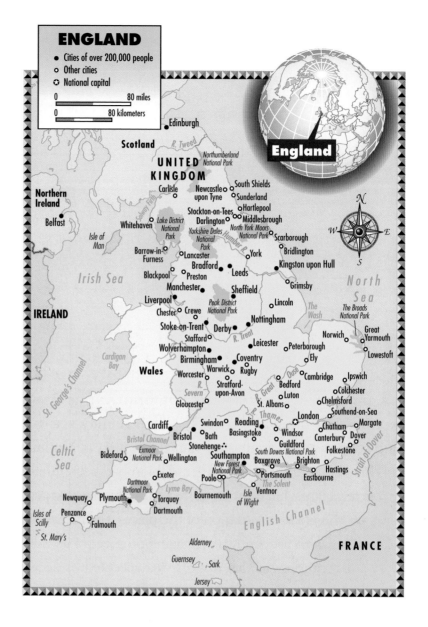

an independent nation. Rather, Great Britain makes up most of the nation called the United Kingdom, or the UK. The fourth part of the United Kingdom is Northern Ireland, the northern portion of the island of Ireland, located to the west of England. England, Scotland, Wales, and Northern Ireland are called the countries of the United Kingdom.

Together, Great Britain and the island of Ireland, along with some small islands offshore, make up the British Isles. England, the British Isles, and the United Kingdom are each also referred to as Britannia. The ancient Romans named this island after Britannia, the Roman goddess of war. Today, Britannia is a symbol of Britain. She appears as a warrior goddess wearing a helmet and carrying a shield and a three-pronged weapon called a trident. She appeared on British coins until 2008.

A statue of Britannia in Liverpool. Britannia is usually depicted as a strong, muscular woman.

English people recognize the general location of a place by the name of the county in which it lies, the way Americans recognize the location of a place by its state. There are more than forty counties in England, but the number has often changed over the years. Many old counties end in the word *shire*, such as Lancashire and Hampshire.

Many parts of Yorkshire are rural.

The smallest county in England is Rutland; it is so tiny that ten Rutlands could fit in the small U.S. state of Rhode Island. The largest English county is Yorkshire. It is so big that it is usually divided into parts—West Riding, East Riding, and North Riding (*Riding* comes from a Norse word meaning "third"). The counties are typically grouped into nine regions: South East, South West, London, East of England, East Midlands, West Midlands, Yorkshire and the Humber, North East, and North West.

Regions and Counties of England

Discovering England

Americans and Canadians visiting England might find what they see, hear, and read to be familiar in many ways. But it can seem very different, too. And that's one of the most interesting parts of getting to know England. The great playwright William Shakespeare called England, "This precious stone set in the silver sea." Come along and learn what makes England unique.

Land and Sea

ENGLAND IS A SMALL COUNTRY, A LITTLE SMALLER than the U.S. state of Alabama. It makes up the southern two-thirds of the island of Great Britain, which is the largest island in Europe. Scotland occupies the land north of the River Tweed and the Cheviot Hills. Wales is the west central part of the island.

Mountains and Lakes

The land in England is lower than any other part of Great Britain. The land in Scotland is much higher. However, England does rise in the middle. The Pennine Mountains run through the center of the country and are often called the backbone of England. In the Pennines, river valleys are called dales. The tops of the Pennines are flat, open land called moors. England's highest point, Scafell Pike, rises 3,210 feet (978 meters) in the Cumbrian Mountains, west of the Pennines.

Scafell Pike is in a part of North West England called the Lake District. Long lakes lie between the peaks in this mountainous area. Windermere, the largest natural lake in England,

England's Geographic Features

Area: 50,346 square miles (130,396 sq km)

Longest Distance North to South: 402 miles (647 km)

Longest Distance East to West: 302 miles (486 km)

Highest Elevation: Scafell Pike, 3,210 feet (978 m) above sea level

Lowest Elevation: Usually sea level, but during low tide near Ely in Cambridgeshire, a small section of exposed land is about 15 feet (5 m) below sea level

Longest River Entirely in England: Thames, 215 miles (346 km) long

Largest Lake: Windermere, 11 miles (18 km) long

Largest Island: Isle of Wight, 147 square miles (381 sq km)

Average High Temperature: In London, 74°F (23°C) in July; 47°F (8°C) in January

Average Low Temperature: In London, 57°F (14°C) in July; 36°F (2°C) in January

Average Annual Rainfall:

East coast	20 inches (51 cm)
Western and northern hills	40 inches (102 cm)
Lake District	130 inches (330 cm)

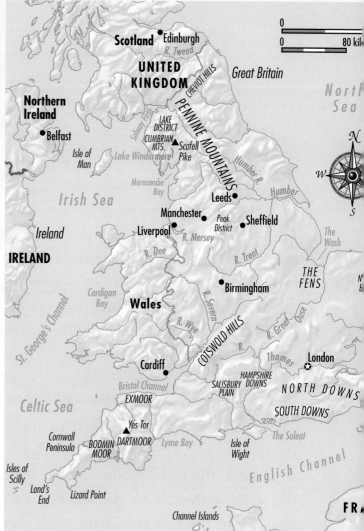

lies in this region. The long, ribbonlike lake is 11 miles (18 kilometers) long but only 1 mile (1.6 km) wide. The Lake District is a popular vacation area and most of it lies within Lake District National Park.

The Coasts

The North Sea, the Irish Sea, and the English Channel surround England. France lies across the English Channel, 21 miles (34 km) from Dover on the south coast. The sea is always nearby in England. In fact, no part of England is more than 68 miles (110 km) from the sea.

Some sections of the White Cliffs of Dover rise 350 feet (110 m) above the water.

The beaches near Newquay attract many visitors. The town's population rises from twenty-two thousand to more than one hundred thousand in the summer.

With 1,150 miles (1,850 km) of coastline, England offers many ways for people to enjoy the water. Most of the sandy beaches are in the South West, in Cornwall and Devon, and the South East, in Kent and Sussex. The water is quite cold for swimming, but the cold doesn't stop hardy English people. The seaside town of Newquay in Cornwall is famous for its surfing. England also has many pebble beaches. On these beaches, seawater gets trapped in pools when the tide goes out. The sea life that lives in the water also gets trapped. People study tide pools on these beaches to see sea life close-up.

Major rivers empty into the sea at the coasts. They form big bays called estuaries, where salty ocean water meets freshwater from the rivers. The biggest estuaries are formed by the Thames in the south, the Humber in the northeast, and the Severn and the Mersey in the west. Major cities developed on these estuaries because they served as ports. Liverpool, for example, is on the Mersey estuary.

England's largest natural harbor is at Poole on the south coast. The only larger natural harbor in the world is Sydney Harbor in Australia.

In other places, the land falls sharply into the sea as great cliffs. England's most famous sea cliffs are the White Cliffs of Dover. These cliffs are located in southeastern England, along the narrowest part of the English Channel. They are the first landmark people see when they are crossing the channel from continental Europe. Cornwall, a peninsula in western England south of Wales, also features great cliffs. The constant battering of the seas wears away the cliffs. People who walk along the cliffs sometimes find places where huge chunks of land have tumbled into the sea.

Raise the Gates

The River Thames runs through London. The river is affected by the tides, so when seas are high or stormy, water can roar down the river, causing great damage to the area. To protect the city, a barrier was built across the river in the 1980s. When high seas and high tides are predicted, floodgates that look like metal sails are raised to keep the river from overflowing its banks.

The Jurassic Coast

In southern England is a 95-mile (153 km) stretch of land called the Jurassic Coast. The rocks that make up the seaside cliffs in this area are exposed. These rocks date back to the Triassic, Jurassic, and Cretaceous periods, the time when dinosaurs dominated the land. Visitors to the coast can see dinosaur footprints and ancient fossilized trees. The geologic history visible along the Jurassic Coast spans 185 million years, ending with the disappearance of dinosaurs 65 million years ago.

The land along the coast northeast of London is wet and low-lying. Called the Fen Country or the Norfolk Broads, the region was first drained by windmills in the 1600s. The windmills pumped excess water out of the land and poured it into the sea. Pumping the land opened it up for farming. Today, electric pumps keep the land dry, but many windmills still stand in the area.

Islands

Hundreds of islands dot the coasts of England. Some, like the Isle of Wight in the south and the Isles of Scilly off Cornwall in the west, are part of England. The Isle of Wight, which lies just off the county of Hampshire, has been a vacation spot since the 1800s. It is renowned for its dramatic coastline. One of its most beautiful sights is the Needles, towering jagged rocks that rise from the sea. The Isles of Scilly include more than fifty islands, but only five are inhabited. Most jobs on the islands are related to tourism.

Open Land

Chalk, a type of soft, white limestone, lies under much of southern England. Chalk formed from the shells of sea creatures that lived more than one hundred million years ago. The White Cliffs of Dover are made of chalk.

Much of the chalk area consists of open hills called downs. Usually only a thin layer of soil forms over chalk, so trees do not grow well. In some places, chalk projects from the soil. Ancient people cut huge figures in the chalk that are still visible today. The oldest chalk figure is the Uffington White Horse, which was created at least three thousand years ago. It is 374 feet (114 m) long and can be seen in full from the air.

The Uffington White Horse can be seen from some places on the ground 20 miles (32 km) away.

Rock outcrops called tors rise above the surrounding land in Dartmoor.

Like chalk downs, moors are open, treeless areas. But unlike the downs, moors have hard rock underneath, and rivers flow across the land. England's three main moors are in southern England. They are Dartmoor in Devon, Exmoor on the Devon border, and Bodmin Moor in Cornwall. In the north, Yorkshire also has moors.

Climate

England is located in the Gulf Stream, a current of warm water that flows from the Caribbean Sea, north past the United States, and across the Atlantic Ocean. The Gulf Stream makes the British Isles much warmer in the winter than other places on the same latitude, such as northern Canada. In the summer, the Gulf Stream water is cooler than the land. This helps keep temperatures in England moderate.

The Highest Village

Flash, in Staffordshire, is the highest village in England. It is located in the Peak District, in central England, at 1,514 feet (461 m) above sea level. It's one of the few places in England that can become snowbound.

July is the warmest month in southern England, but even then the high temperature is often below 70°F (21°C).

Rain falls an average of 145 days a year in London.

The Gulf Stream brings moisture and warmth to England, helping keep it green all year long. The Lake District in the North West gets the most rain of anywhere in England, about 130 inches (330 cm) each year. An average of only 20 inches (50 cm) of rain falls in London each year.

In London, snow usually falls a few days each winter. Regions farther north get more snow. The Lake District and other hilly areas in the north have ski runs.

The warmest areas are along the coasts. Portsmouth, for example, reaches an average high of 49 degrees Fahrenheit (9 degrees Celsius) in January and 72°F (22°C) in July. In England, anything above 75°F (24°C) is considered a heat wave. The highest temperature ever recorded in England was 101.3°F (38.5°C), at Brogdale in Kent, on August 10, 2003.

Big Cities

London, England's capital city, is also its largest city, with a population of more than 8 million people. The West Midlands is the second most populated area after London, and at its heart is the city of Birmingham. In 2010, Birmingham was home to more than 1 million people. Birmingham began as a settlement in the sixth or seventh century CE. By medieval times, it was a market town. The city grew in importance as manufacturing grew, first in small family workshops and later in big factories. Today, Birmingham is the center of England's high-tech and automotive industries.

Liverpool is the third-largest city in England, with a population of around 816,200 people. Much of the city's waterfront (below) has been designated a World Heritage Site by the United Nations because of its historic ports on the Mersey Estuary. In the nineteenth century, it was the busiest port in the world. Ships moved in and

out of the port weighed down with cargo. Many Irish people left for America from Liverpool. Today, Liverpool is an important cultural and educational center.

The next largest cities—Leeds (population 810,200) and Sheffield (population 640,720)—are in the county of Yorkshire. Both are important industrial cities. For a long time, Leeds was an important wool-processing city. In more recent years, the city has produced furniture, paper, and electrical equipment. It is also a transportation hub, with many railway lines passing through it.

Sheffield (above) has long been known for its steel products. It is located on six rivers, and it is said that the rivers "powered the wheels that ground the steel that made Sheffield famous." Part of the city lies within the Peak District National Park, and the city is filled with gardens and woods. Sheffield has more trees per person than any other city in Europe.

Natural England

P

EOPLE HAVE BEEN MAKING USE OF THE LAND IN England for so long that there are few totally "natural," or untouched, places left. Across the land, people have cut down trees, built villages, and drained soggy lands to make farms. However, there still is plenty of green space in England.

Many English people love walking, and they take advantage of a system of walking paths called National Trails. Thirteen different National Trails total more than 2,500 miles (4,000 km). Offa's Dyke Path runs along the border with Wales along an earthwork built in the eighth century. The South West Coast Path is 630 miles (1,014 km) long and takes a walker completely around Dorset, Cornwall, and Devon.

Opposite: **The South West Coast Path is the longest marked path in England.**

Mammals

Britain was once a land of many big animals, including aurochs (a type of ox), brown bears, gray wolves, and even cave lions. Cave lions disappeared from England about ten

Hippos in England

Hippopotamuses once lived on the land that is now England. That was about 125,000 years ago, when the planet was warmer, seas were higher, and Great Britain was attached to the rest of Europe. In 2004, the bones of hippopotamuses much larger than modern-day ones were found in Suffolk, near the North Sea.

thousand years ago. Giant elephantine creatures called woolly mammoths died off at about the same time.

Male red deer have antlers, which they shed each year. The antlers can grow 1 inch (2.5 cm) a day.

The mammals that live in England today are few in kind but number many. The largest land animal in England is the red deer. It has a long tail and is found primarily in the Lake District

in the North West and in Exmoor in Cornwall. The most common deer is the fallow deer, which is much smaller than the red deer. Most fallow deer have spots on their coats. The roe deer of the West Country is small and reddish-brown in color.

Foxes are common throughout England. They live all across the country, on farms, in woods, and in towns. Otters swim in rivers, while seals, dolphins, and other sea mammals make their homes near the coasts. Badgers are shy animals that are rarely seen. Even though they often live near people, they spend most of their time underground and come out only at night. The smallest mammal in England is the harvest mouse, which lives in fields.

Ponies have lived in the wilds of Dartmoor, Exmoor, and the New Forest, which lies mostly in Hampshire, for hundreds

Red foxes have excellent hearing. They can hear mice and other prey under the ground.

of years. The ones in Dartmoor are the descendants of ponies that were used in tin mines in the area. But the Exmoor and New Forest ponies are native breeds that have existed for more than a thousand years. The Exmoor ponies are in danger of becoming extinct. None of these ponies are truly wild. Pony keepers look after them and make sure they don't starve.

Birds

England has a wide variety of environments that attract many different kinds of birds. There are more than five hundred bird species in Great Britain, and most of them are found in England.

Exmoor ponies are strong and sturdy.

Hedgerows and Hedgehogs

Looking a bit like a pinecone on legs, the hedgehog is a small mammal that can roll up into a prickly ball to protect itself when startled. Hedgehogs often live in hedgerows. These are rows of shrubs and trees originally planted to mark the edges of farm fields. Many hedgerows were planted hundreds of years ago. They are home to various kinds of wildlife, especially birds. In recent years, a lot of hedgerows have been removed so that farm machinery can be used more efficiently on fields.

The red grouse, one of the few birds that stay in one place year-round, lives on open moorland. Hunters often prey on this plump, medium-sized bird.

Many other birds come from mainland Europe or Africa for part of the year. Elegant white swans breed in England. They normally live in pairs near rivers and ponds, which they claim as their own.

The English robin is the national bird of the United Kingdom. It bears little resemblance to the American robin, though it does have an orange-red breast. The American robin was named after the English robin because both birds have red breasts.

One of the glories of being outdoors in England is the chance to hear a skylark. The male skylark soars into the sky and sings a beautiful song that echoes for miles. The English poet Percy Bysshe Shelley celebrated this beloved bird in his poem "Ode to a Skylark." Sadly, the number of skylarks is

Robin Hood's Oak

England has many ancient trees. One of the most famous is the Major Oak in Sherwood Forest in Nottinghamshire, where, legend says, Robin Hood and his Merry Men hid out. The tree is thought to be at least eight hundred years old. At ground level, the distance around the outside of the trunk is about 34 feet (10 m). Some branches are so huge and heavy they need support poles under them to keep them from breaking.

dropping drastically because they search for food in farm fields that have been treated with poisons to kill pests.

Trees, Plants, and Flowers

England has many green spots that provide people with the opportunity to get away from crowded cities. Moors are quiet, treeless, grassy areas that drain well. England also has areas of shrubland called heaths, which have acidic soil that doesn't drain so well. Heather grows well on the heath, and its abundant flowers give the landscape its delicate purple appearance.

Forests are rare in England. Most of the forests lie in the South East. The most common trees in Britain are oak, elm, ash, and beech. Wildflowers, however, are very common. Red poppies, yellow daffodils, purple irises, white daisies, and many, many more flowers brighten the land.

Preserving Nature

England has set aside ten areas as national parks. By creating national parks, the government hopes to help preserve the natural beauty of the land, help protect the animals that live there, and encourage the public to appreciate the land.

England's national parks include Lake District National Park (below) and the Peak District National Park, which are near each other in the north. The Lake District park features beautiful lakes that were gouged out by retreating glaciers long ago. The Peak District park features the rugged hills of the northern Pennine Mountains. Northumberland National Park, on the border with Scotland, is home to Hadrian's Wall, built by the ancient Romans.

South Downs National Park, the country's youngest national park, began operating in 2011. It protects the white chalk that makes the downs, including the White Cliffs of Dover. A national trail 99 miles (160 km) long runs through the park.

Some places in England are designated Areas of Outstanding Natural Beauty (AONBs) and Sites of Special Scientific Interest (SSSIs). There are almost forty AONBs in England. They range from the Cotswolds (above), a region of beautiful small villages, to Chichester Harbour, one of the natural sections of the south coast.

An SSSI can be a nature reserve, a geological site, or a breeding ground for a species. England has hundreds of SSSIs. In Cheshire, for example, a wetland with rare mosses is designated as an SSSI. The largest SSSI in England is the Wash, an area of Norfolk and Lincolnshire that consists of a huge bay and estuary and the low-lying marshy fens around it.

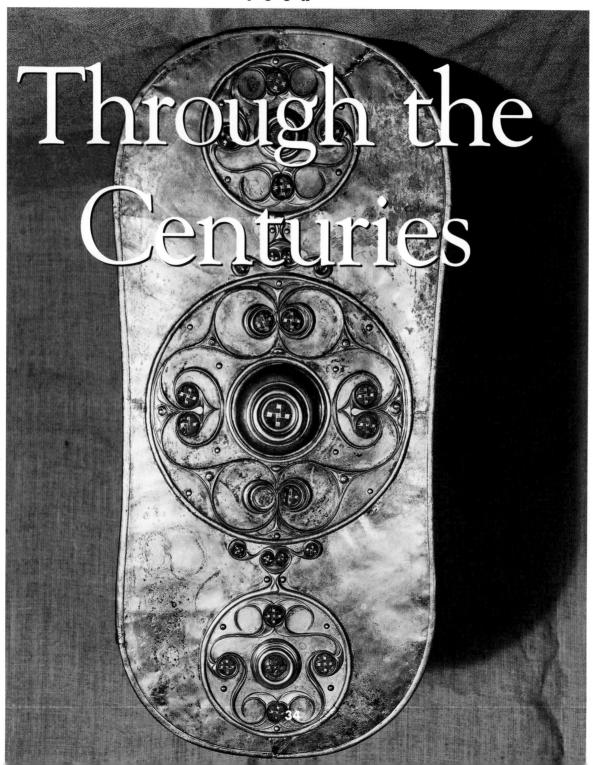

Through the Centuries

THE FIRST PEOPLE TO OCCUPY ENGLAND WERE probably farmers. More than five thousand years ago, people made their way across the English Channel from continental Europe in search of good lands to farm. The climate was gentler on Great Britain than on the continent, so they stayed. Archaeologists—scientists who study the remains of past cultures—know about these farmers from the huge burial mounds they built, called barrows. These people also built huge circles of stones, perhaps for religious reasons. The most famous of these is Stonehenge.

Opposite: **People have been living in the area that is now London for more than two thousand years. The Battersea Shield, found in the River Thames in 1857, was made between 350 and 50 BCE.**

Early Peoples

About the same time that stone circles were first being constructed, a different group of people began to arrive in England. Little is known about them except that they made cups of a distinctive shape, earning them the name the Beaker People. These people started mining tin in Cornwall and traded it on the continent.

Ancient Stonehenge

On the Salisbury Plain southwest of London is a great circle of upright stones. Called Stonehenge, it is one of the world's greatest prehistoric sites. About 5,300 years ago, people created a huge earthen circle on the land. Later, stones were added. The large stones weigh about 50 tons (45 metric tons) each. No one knows for sure why Stonehenge was built. A line of stones follows the exact line of sunrise on June 21, the summer solstice, the day of the year when the sun is up for the longest time. This precise arrangement of the stones makes some people think Stonehenge was an astronomical observatory.

Another people began to spread throughout Europe about 600 or 700 BCE. The Celts (pronounced *kelts*) reached England about 450 BCE. They brought with them the ability to work with iron, and thus started the British Iron Age. The Celts were divided into extended family groups called clans. Various clans built hill forts. These were protected hilltops where people could be safe from attack. The language of the Celts formed the basis of the Irish, Welsh, and Scottish languages. But in most of England, the Celtic language and culture were pushed aside by Roman invaders and then the Angles and Saxons.

Outpost of the Roman Empire

The ancient Romans ruled an empire that was based in what is now Italy. Their empire spread over much of western Europe, northern Africa, and western Asia. The Romans wanted to expand their empire as far westward as they could. The point farthest west that they could reach was the island they called Pretani. That name became Britanni. When the Roman ruler Julius Caesar first attempted to take the island in 54 BCE, the Roman army was not strong enough. But in 43 CE, Roman soldiers under Emperor Claudius conquered the Celtic people who lived there. They took possession of the southern part of the island—the area that is now England. The Pictish people, who lived in the north in what is now Scotland, were never conquered. The Romans built two walls to keep the Picts out of their Roman province of Britannia. Construction on the first, Hadrian's Wall, began in 122 CE and took about six years. The second, Antonine Wall, was built about two decades later.

Roman Conquest of Britain

Roman control, 43–47 CE		Defensive wall	
Roman control, 49–78 CE		Fort	
Roman control, 79 CE		Settlement	
Roman control, 80 CE		Iceni	Tribe

The Romans intended to stay permanently. The soldiers moved their families to the island. Other soldiers married local women. Cities and roads were built. Generation after generation grew up in Britannia. Tribal people who were captured in battle served as slaves to the Romans. For the Romans, life was good.

Finding Rome in England

In Somerset County about 100 miles (160 km) west of London are large natural hot springs, where hot water bubbles up from beneath the ground. The Celtic people who lived in the area two thousand years ago dedicated the hot springs to a goddess named Sulis. After the Romans invaded, they built a town on the site, which they called Aquae Sulis, meaning "the waters of Sulis." The Romans built a temple and elaborate bathing complex on the site.

After the Romans left England, the bathing complex fell into ruin. Centuries later, a new bathing complex was built in the town now called Bath. Some areas of old Roman Baths have been excavated, and a museum holds columns, carvings, and other artifacts of the town's Roman past. More remnants of ancient Rome are still being discovered there. In 2012, a stash of more than thirty thousand Roman coins was discovered not far from the Roman Baths.

Some tribal people continued to fight. The Iceni, for example, were a Celtic tribe in East Anglia (now Norfolk). One of their leaders was a woman named Boudicca. She took on the Roman troops and even burned Londinium, the early settlement of London. The Romans put down the rebellion, however.

The Roman Empire faced increasing troubles in the following centuries. On the continent, tribes from the north and east were weakening Roman defenses. Rome could no longer pay much attention to its distant provinces. Trade between Britannia and the continent dropped off. Soldiers and government officials were recalled to Rome. Many of them refused to return to the continent because they did not consider Rome their home. Their ancestors had been in Britannia for generations. The Romans left Britannia by 410, but the influence of their culture carried on. Their language—Latin—remained the language used for doing business in England for another thousand years.

New Peoples Arrive

Britannia was weakened with the departure of the Romans. Tribes from the continent began to invade. The Angles, Saxons, and Jutes all came from Germany after the Roman defenses were gone. Many historians think these peoples didn't attack, but came peacefully, planning to settle in the area.

Boudicca set fire to the city of Londinium so that the Romans could not keep control of it.

The Legend of King Arthur

Sometime in the early years of the Saxon invasion, a leader called King Arthur helped defend the English lands. He became a hero to his people. That is about all that is known of the real King Arthur. But legends about him began to develop almost immediately. In the twelfth century, Geoffrey of Monmouth created most of the stories told about Arthur today. He wrote about the Round Table, the sword Excalibur, and Merlin the magician. French writer Chrétien de Troyes expanded the story of King Arthur. He added Lancelot, as well as the idea that the Holy Grail—the cup Jesus is said to have drunk from shortly before he died—might be in England.

Whatever happened, the different tribes set up small kingdoms in England. Their cultures gradually replaced the Celtic culture. The people who lived in southern Great Britain became Anglo-Saxons, and their languages merged and developed into the new language of Angle-ish, or English.

The Viking Invasion

More invaders came, starting about 840. These invaders, called Norsemen or Vikings, were from Scandinavia. They sailed up English rivers and captured villages and land. They destroyed Christian monasteries, where religious people lived and devoted their lives to God, and stole the monasteries' riches. Soon, the Vikings had control of central England, a region they called the Danelaw. But Alfred, king of the West Saxons, or Wessex, began to fight back. He succeeded at ousting the Vikings, which eventually earned him the name Alfred the Great.

Starting in 927, Athelstan, king of Wessex and Mercia, gathered several kingdoms under his control, primarily by making political alliances. He created a unified kingdom in 936 and became the first real king of England. But the England he knew didn't last.

The Norman Conquest

In 1066, Normans from across the English Channel invaded and captured England. The Normans were descended from the Norsemen who, a hundred years before, had taken control of land that is now part of France. The Normans, under Duke William of Normandy, were ready to expand. At the Battle of Hastings, the Norman forces conquered the army of King Harold II of England. Duke William became known as William the Conqueror and was crowned king of England on Christmas Day, 1066.

William created a system of aristocracy, or inherited titles and land, that still exists today. He took land away from the Saxons and gave it to about 180 barons, who then passed some land on to their knights. The knights, in turn, gave some land

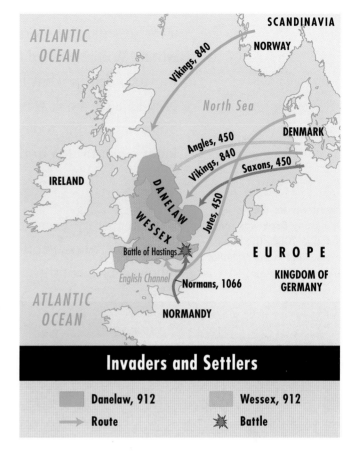

Invaders and Settlers

- Danelaw, 912
- Route
- Wessex, 912
- Battle

away to serfs, and soon no one knew which land belonged to whom. William called for an accounting of land ownership. It was recorded in what is called the *Domesday Book*. This "day of judgment" book was used to settle landownership disputes. Some aristocrats today still bear the names—and own the lands—mentioned in the book a thousand years ago.

The survey for the *Domesday Book* was completed in 1086. The book is now kept in the National Archives in London.

History by Kings

English history became a history of kings, because they are the people whose stories were recorded. Henrys and Edwards followed one another, sometimes fighting over succession, or

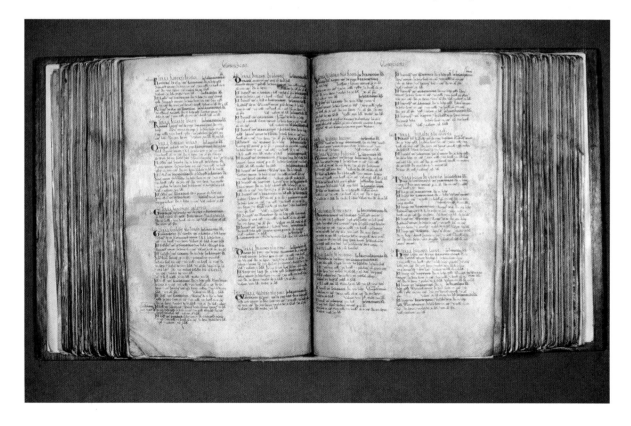

who would become the next king. Kings often dragged the common people into their quarrels, but sometimes the people were able to change history. That happened with King John in 1215.

King John's barons were angry for many reasons, mostly about money and position. They forced John to sign a paper called the Magna Carta, meaning "great charter." This paper stated that the king's power was limited, and that he must act according to the laws of the land rather than his own whim. John signed the Magna Carta, but he didn't keep to the agreement. Nonetheless, the Magna Carta is often seen as a forerunner of the U.S. Constitution.

For thirty years, the English fought each other in the Wars of the Roses, which were wars of succession. Henry VI of the Lancaster family, whose symbol was a red rose, took the throne away from Richard II of the York family, whose symbol

King John signed the Magna Carta in 1215. This was the first time English people had forced their king to sign a document.

The Black Death

The plague was one of the most horrific epidemics in human history. Known as the Black Death, it started in Asia and quickly spread across Europe. It reached England in 1348, and in two years it is estimated to have killed half of all the people who lived there. The disease was terrifying. It caused swelling that looked like large blisters. People would get high fevers and vomit blood. They would die within a few days of being infected.

was a white rose. The wars ended in 1485, when the last York, Richard III, was killed in battle by forces led by a Lancaster relative named Henry Tudor.

The Tudors

Henry Tudor became Henry VII and started a new line of kings. Because Henry was Welsh, he unified England and Wales as one nation. He sent explorers to look into the new lands that had been discovered across the Atlantic Ocean. John Cabot and his son Sebastian found fabulous fishing grounds off Newfoundland, which Cabot claimed for England. Newfoundland is now part of Canada.

Henry Tudor's son and successor Henry VIII changed England drastically, through religion. England was a Catholic country, and the Catholic Church did not allow divorce. Henry VIII broke with the Roman Catholic Church so he could get divorced. In 1534, the Church of England became the official church of the land, and Henry was its leader.

Henry's daughter, Queen Elizabeth I, became one of the most memorable monarchs in English history. She sent explorers to North America. Her favorite sailor, Francis Drake, became the first Englishman to sail around the world. Drake returned to England a wealthy man from attacking Spanish ships that carried gold from the Americas. These attacks angered the Spanish, who wanted to overthrow Elizabeth I. They sent a huge fleet of ships, called the Spanish Armada, to fight against England in 1588. Bad weather and an attack by English ships drove off the Spanish Armada.

Monarchs In and Out

Queen Elizabeth died in 1603, and James I became king. He was certain he had a divine right to be king and could do what he wanted. Parliament, the kingdom's legislature, didn't agree.

Becoming the United Kingdom

1485 Henry Tudor of Wales becomes Henry VII of England, uniting England and Wales.

1541 Henry VIII (left) forces the Irish to acknowledge him as their king.

1603 Elizabeth I dies without children. Parliament brings King James Stuart of Scotland, a descendant of Henry VII, to England, making him James I.

1707 The Acts of Union join Scotland to England and Wales.

1801 Great Britain and Ireland join to form the United Kingdom of Great Britain and Ireland.

1921 Under the Anglo-Irish Treaty, two-thirds of the island of Ireland becomes independent. The northern counties, called Northern Ireland, remain part of the United Kingdom.

When James's son, Charles I, came to power, he also believed he had the divine right to rule, and his conflict with Parliament resulted in a civil war. Charles was eventually beheaded.

Oliver Cromwell, as head of Parliament's army, took charge of the nation, naming himself Lord Protector of what he called the Commonwealth of England. Cromwell was a Puritan. Puritans believed that the Church of England needed to be "purified," or rid of its Roman Catholic beliefs and practices. Cromwell's armies destroyed many churches. After

Oliver Cromwell had no military experience when the English Civil War began. He quickly rose through the ranks, however, to become the leader of the parliamentary army.

The Great Fire

In 1666, the Great Fire of London swept through the city. The fire raged for four days, destroying more than thirteen thousand houses, along with nearly ninety churches and many government buildings. After the fire, the city was rebuilt with the same street plan, and buildings were reconstructed on the same sites. But rather than being made from wood, the buildings were made from brick and stone, which do not burn. Architect Christopher Wren made a permanent mark on the city by designing fifty-one new churches to replace those that had been destroyed.

Cromwell's death in 1658, the commonwealth quickly fell apart. The people insisted that the monarchy be restored.

In 1685, James II was crowned king. James was Catholic, and he tried to keep Roman Catholics safe from persecution. But many people in England did not want a Catholic to be king. In what was known as the Glorious Revolution, Parliament invited William of Orange, the husband of James's daughter, to bring an army from the Netherlands to force James off the throne. The plan was to then have William become king of England. William succeeded, and he and his wife, Mary, a Protestant, became joint rulers in 1689.

Parliament had to bring another monarch from the continent in 1714, when there was no direct heir to the throne. They brought George I from Germany, starting the Hanover line of kings. Today's monarch, Queen Elizabeth II, is a descendant of George I.

The British ruled India for nearly two hundred years.

England Abroad

Having gained a fierce reputation from destroying the Spanish Armada and as a result of its many explorations across oceans, England became a world power. The English built colonies in North America. They touched on the edges of New Zealand and Australia. They formed the East India Company to explore the Indian Ocean and begin trade with India and other areas of South Asia. The British controlled lands all across the globe. By the end of the nineteenth century, they could proudly proclaim, "The sun never sets on the British Empire."

Starting in 1660, the English engaged in the slave trade. English merchants bought black Africans and transported them to the colonies in North America to sell as slaves.

George III was king in 1775 when the American colonies rebelled at being governed by a distant land that gave them no voice in decisions. English soldiers traveled to America to fight, but they lost the war. The colonies formed a new nation, the United States of America.

Queen Victoria, granddaughter of George III, took the throne in 1837. She remained on the throne until her death in 1901. Her sixty-four year reign is the longest in British history. During her long reign, which became known as the Victorian Era, England's businesspeople and soldiers formed many new colonies. The House of Commons became more powerful than the aristocrats of the House of Lords. Scientific exploration and invention blossomed in ways that affected the entire world.

British Empire, 1919

Britain and possessions — Present-day borders

Abraham Darby III designed the world's first iron structure, a bridge near the iron foundry started by his grandfather. The bridge was built between 1777 and 1779.

The Industrial Revolution

English society had changed greatly in the preceding century. Much of this was due to what is called the Industrial Revolution, which began in England. This was a time when technological advances flourished.

English people revolutionized the way iron is obtained. Iron had been used for thousands of years, but extracting the useful metal from its ore was a slow process. In 1709, Abraham Darby found that he could make large quantities of iron by smelting (cooking) the ore with coke, a coal that has been roasted to remove the oxygen in it. When coke is mixed with the melted iron ore, oxygen leaves the ore and joins the coke, leaving free iron.

Iron is the basis of industry. It is used for making machinery, which produces other products. It is also used for making steam engines, which power the machinery. James Watt of Scotland developed the steam engine.

A model of James Watt's steam engine. Steam engines powered the Industrial Revolution.

Workers at a textile factory in Manchester. Manchester was the center of England's cotton industry in the 1800s.

England also led the world in the development of factories. In the 1700s, several mills were built. There, cotton thread was spun and woven. The flowing waters of the River Derwent in central England powered these mills. Factories began employing enough people on different work shifts to keep the looms going day and night. A businessman named Richard Arkwright developed machinery so that spinning did not require skilled workers.

Soon, more mills were built. People poured out from the countryside into the cities to work at the mills. As more and more factories were built, cities grew. England was no longer a country of farmers.

James Watt's steam engine powered railroads as well as factories. In 1801, Richard Trevithick of Cornwall made a steam-powered vehicle that ran on rails for use in mines. Two decades later, George Stephenson built the world's first public railroad. A steam-powered locomotive pulled the train 26 miles (42 km) in northeastern England. Soon Great Britain was covered by thousands of miles of railroad tracks, most of them converging on London.

Isambard Kingdom Brunel used the idea of the big steam engine to power the world's first steamship. The *Great Western* crossed the Atlantic Ocean in 1838. Soon Britain was the major shipping company of the world.

The Stockton and Darlington Railway opened in 1825 in northeastern England. It was the world's first public passenger and freight railway.

The United Kingdom took the lead in two wars in the twentieth century. In World War I (1914–1918), allies led by the United Kingdom, France, Russia, and later, the United States, fought Germany and Austria-Hungary. Almost a million British soldiers were killed during the war.

Meanwhile, many people in Ireland were eager to be free of British rule. In 1921, the island was partitioned. Northern Ireland remained part of the United Kingdom. The rest of Ireland became the Irish Free State and, later, the Republic of Ireland.

British soldiers in the trenches during World War I. The trenches provided protection from enemy fire.

In 1939, Europe became engulfed in war again when World War II started. Germany, under Adolf Hitler, was taking over neighboring countries. In what came to be called the Battle of Britain, Germany bombed the UK in 1940 in an attempt to force the British out of the war. German missiles destroyed much of London. Almost every nation in the world was involved in World War II by the time it ended in 1945.

Bombing raids during World War II left London in ruins. By May 1941, more than a million houses in the city had been damaged or destroyed.

After the War

England had suffered heavy damage during the war, both physically and financially. When the war ended, bombed areas had to be rebuilt, but the country's finances were depleted. The United States helped England rebuild.

In the years after the war, all of the United Kingdom's remaining colonies became independent. People from many of these former colonies moved to England. Immigrants came to England from India, Pakistan, Jamaica, Bangladesh, and other countries around the world. The face of England was changing.

Britain joined other European nations in forming the organization that became the European Union, or EU. By combining forces economically and politically, these countries were able to help one another and have more influence together than each would alone. Many EU countries began using the same currency, called the euro, but the United Kingdom voted to continue using its traditional currency, the pound sterling.

In 1948, England had a labor shortage and began encouraging immigration. Large numbers of Jamaicans moved to England in search of work.

Building for the Olympics

The Olympic Games have been held in London three times: 1908, 1948, and 2012. It is the only city to have hosted the games so many times.

When London was chosen as the site of the 2012 Summer Olympics, the British government used the opportunity to revitalize much of the East End of London, especially the section called Stratford. It built a new stadium (left) and a village called Queen Elizabeth Olympic Park. The village held more than seventeen thousand athletes and officials during the Olympics. There are plans to convert the village into housing for up to five thousand families.

Troubled Times

On July 6, 2005, English people were excited to learn that London had been selected as the site of the 2012 Olympic Summer Games. But the very next day, there was a suicide bombing by four young Muslim Englishmen who set off explosives on London buses and subway trains. In addition to the bombers, fifty-two other people were killed, and hundreds of others were injured.

In 2008, the global economy went into a steep decline. This downturn hit England hard. The economic crisis prompted the government to rein in spending. In 2011, the government began cutting the number of government workers. It also required workers to pay more toward their pensions, money that they will receive after they retire. When the government announced that budget cuts would go on until at least 2017, public employees—which includes health care workers and teachers—protested by stopping work. It was the biggest strike in Britain in a generation.

Monarchs and Ministers

T HE GOVERNMENT OF ENGLAND IS A PARLIAMENTARY democracy. That means that Parliament—the legislature—chooses the prime minister, who is the head of government. The people elect members of Parliament.

England also has a monarch—a king or queen—who is the head of state. For hundreds of years, the monarch actually ruled, deciding how the nation was to be run. But during that time, the British Parliament gradually took away some of the monarch's powers. Today, in addition to being a parliamentary democracy, England, and the United Kingdom as a whole, is a constitutional monarchy. The monarch can do only those things that the laws allow. Today, the duties and activities of the monarch are mainly ceremonial. The monarch is not allowed to express political opinions.

Opposite: **Queen Elizabeth II is the head of state in England. She opens the session of Parliament every year during an elaborate ceremony.**

The Biggest Audience

On April 29, 2011, Prince William married Catherine Middleton, who is called Kate, at Westminster Abbey in London. An estimated two billion people worldwide watched the event on television, and hundreds of millions more watched it live on the Internet.

The Monarchy

England's monarch today is Queen Elizabeth II, who has been queen since 1952. In June 2012, the country celebrated her sixtieth year on the throne with a Diamond Jubilee. The queen lives in Buckingham Palace in London, but that is not her official residence. The official residence is Windsor Castle, about 20 miles (32 km) away in Berkshire.

The heir to the throne is Elizabeth's oldest son, Prince Charles. After Charles, the heir is Prince William, his older son.

England's Flag

The flag of England is called St. George's Cross. It consists of a red cross on a white background. St. George is the patron saint of England. He was a Roman soldier from about 300 CE who was persecuted for becoming a Christian. Legend says that St. George slew a dragon, perhaps near the town of Glastonbury, although there is no evidence that he was ever in England—or that dragons have ever existed.

The Union Jack is the official flag of the United Kingdom. It is red, white, and blue with a red cross through the center. It is a combination of the national flags of England, Scotland, and Ireland.

In 2011, the British changed the centuries-old Act of Settlement, which required that a monarch's oldest son be heir to the throne. Now, the first child—boy or girl—born to Prince William will be heir to the throne. The law was also changed to allow the monarch to marry a Roman Catholic.

Buckingham Palace is the queen's home in London and the center of the British monarchy. It has 775 rooms.

Parliament

England's government is the United Kingdom's government. Since 1999, the other countries in the United Kingdom—Wales, Scotland, and Northern Ireland—have had governing assemblies that deal with situations within their own regions. England, however, does not have a legislature apart from Parliament.

Big Ben

Both bodies of Parliament meet in the Houses of Parliament in London. The wing that holds the House of Commons was destroyed during World War II, but it was rebuilt following the original plans. A tall clock tower rises from the Houses of Parliament. The clock is known as Big Ben and is one of the symbols of London.

Two bodies make up the national Parliament. The House of Lords is smaller and less representative of the people than the House of Commons. The House of Lords used to include only people who were lords by inheritance—the aristocrats, or nobility, who are also called peers of the realm—as well as leaders in the Church of England. But that has changed in recent years. Today, the House of Lords includes only 90 hereditary peers among its 790 members. The rest of the members are life peers. They are appointed by the queen for their achievements. Their titles die with them rather than being passed on to their children.

Female First

The first woman to serve in Parliament was Nancy Astor, an American who was born Nancy Langhorne. She was married to Waldorf Astor, an Englishman, who was a Member of Parliament (MP). When he entered the House of Lords, his wife ran for his seat in the House of Commons and won. She was an MP from 1919 to 1945.

The members of the House of Commons, called MPs, for Members of Parliament, are elected by the public. There are 650 MPs, and about 590 of them are from England.

The Ministers

The political party that wins the most seats in Parliament chooses the prime minister. The prime minister is in charge of the overall direction of the government. He or she chooses a cabinet from among the MPs. Each cabinet minister is in charge of policy in a different area, such as foreign affairs or education. The prime minister must appear in Parliament regularly to answer questions. Those question sessions can get very rowdy.

Prime Minister David Cameron answers questions in Parliament. He became prime minister in 2010.

If the members of Parliament disapprove of how the prime minister is doing the job, they can hold a vote saying they have no confidence in him or her. They choose a new prime minister if the prime minister loses the no-confidence vote. If the parties cannot agree on a new prime minister, a new general election must be held for all the seats in the House of Commons. Any citizen at least eighteen years old can vote.

In 2011, a law was passed that set specific terms for general elections for the first time. There will be an election on May 7, 2015, and then elections will be held every five years thereafter. Still, an election could be held sooner if a new government can't be formed or if the House votes in favor of holding a new election.

The Iron Lady

No woman had ever been prime minister in the United Kingdom until Margaret Thatcher (1925–) led the Conservative Party to power in 1979. Thatcher was the daughter of a grocer. She attended Oxford University, where she became active in conservative politics. She was first elected to Parliament in 1959 and quickly became known for her strong conservative beliefs. She argued in favor of lower taxes and supported capital punishment. As education secretary in the early 1970s, she supported cuts in spending.

As prime minister, she continued these policies. She cut taxes, slashed spending on education and other programs, limited the power of trade unions, and sold government businesses such as the gas, water, and electric industries to private companies. Together, her policies became known as Thatcherism. Because of her uncompromising beliefs and tough personality, people called her the Iron Lady.

Local Government

England is divided up into counties. Most are run by county councils, which generally function in areas outside cities. Some places have governments called unitary authorities, which means that one government runs both a city and the rural areas around it. Local governments are responsible for issues relating to education, roads, and parks.

The Courts

Since October 2009, the United Kingdom has had a Supreme Court, which has twelve professional judges. The Supreme Court cannot overturn laws created by Parliament, but it can

Voters go to a polling station in London. English citizens must be at least eighteen years old to vote.

A Closer Look at London

London, England's capital and largest city, is one of the world's leading cities. It is a center of culture, finance, education, fashion, and more. London began as the Roman settlement of Londinium and gradually grew into a large city, with an estimated population of sixty thousand. The city shrank for a time after the Romans left, but then began to flourish again, becoming a center for business and politics. For much of the 1800s, London was the largest city in the world.

Today, London is a bustling, multicultural city, where more than three hundred different languages are spoken. More than eight million people live within the city limits. About fourteen million live in the city and its suburbs,

making it the largest metropolitan area in the European Union. With so many people living in the area, traffic in central London became very congested. To help improve the situation, a fee system was put in place in 2003. Cars going into central London on weekdays must pay a fee that equals about $15.00 a day. Cameras mounted around the area record the license plate number of every car that enters. Computers then check whether the owner of that car has paid the fee. Since the fees were enacted, traffic going into central London has dropped by about 35 percent.

London is a city of big parks as well as skyscrapers. Together, Hyde Park (left, bottom) and Kensington Gardens splash a large swath of green across central London. The tallest building in London was completed in 2012. The Shard London Bridge (left, top), also known as the Shard (meaning a sharp piece of glass, which the building resembles), used to be called London Bridge Tower. It is 1,017 feet (310 m) tall, making it the tallest building in England and in the entire European Union.

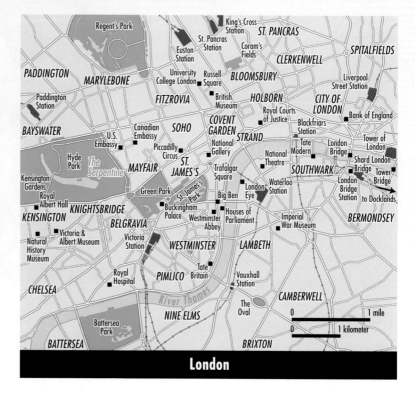

London

force Parliament to reconsider any laws that affect human rights. The court also hears appeals of cases from the courts of England and Wales, Northern Ireland, and Scotland. A panel of five judges hears most cases.

Most criminal cases begin in a Magistrates' Court. If someone believes a judge made an error in the case, he or she can

National Anthem

"God Save the Queen" is the national anthem of the United Kingdom. The song has existed for several hundred years, but no one knows who wrote it or when it was written. It uses the same tune as the American patriotic song "God Bless America." "God Save the Queen" has several verses, but typically only the first verse is sung. Until recent years, it was sung at the end of all public gatherings. The word *Queen* is changed to *King*, depending on who England's monarch is at the time.

> God save our gracious Queen,
> Long live our noble Queen,
> God save the Queen.
> Send her victorious,
> Happy and glorious,
> Long to reign over us;
> God save the Queen.

ask the Crown Court or the High Court to review the case. These courts also try some cases directly. Further appeals can be made to the Court of Appeal or the Supreme Court.

The International Scene

The United Kingdom joined the European Union in 1973. The EU's legislative branch is made up of two groups: the European Parliament and the Council of the European Union. The European Parliament is made up of representatives, who are elected every five years. In 2012, the European Parliament had 754 members. Sixty-four of them came from the UK. The

National Government of the United Kingdom

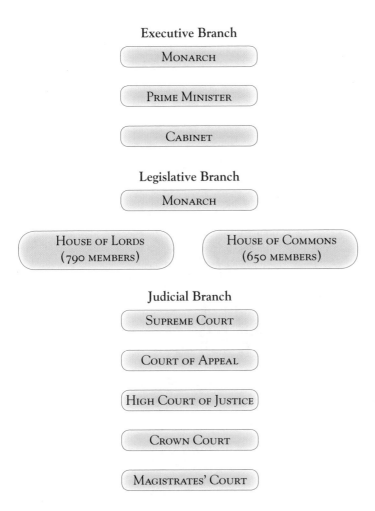

Executive Branch

Monarch

Prime Minister

Cabinet

Legislative Branch

Monarch

House of Lords
(790 members)

House of Commons
(650 members)

Judicial Branch

Supreme Court

Court of Appeal

High Court of Justice

Crown Court

Magistrates' Court

Council is made up of ministers from each member state. All proposals for laws must come from the European Commission, the executive branch of the EU. The European Parliament and the Council can approve, reject, or change the proposed laws. They also control the budget for the EU.

CHAPTER SIX

The World of Work

THE INDUSTRIAL REVOLUTION BEGAN IN THE UNITED Kingdom in the 1700s, and in the 1800s the country was the world's dominant economic power. Although by the late 1800s its power had declined, today the United Kingdom still has the seventh-largest economy in the world. And England has the largest economy of any of the four parts of the nation.

Opposite: **A farmer plows a field in Wiltshire. Most English farms are small, less than 250 acres (100 hectares).**

Agriculture and Fishing

Only about 2 percent of the British workforce is employed in agriculture, but English farmers can supply three-fifths of England's food needs. England's chief crops are wheat, sugar beets, barley, potatoes, and oil rapeseed. Much of the wheat and barley is used for animal feed. England has rich grazing land for cattle and sheep. Pigs and poultry are also raised there.

What the United Kingdom Grows, Makes, and Mines

Agriculture (2009)

Wheat	14,379,000 metric tons
Milk	13,236,500 metric tons
Sugar beets	8,330,000 metric tons

Manufacturing (value added by manufacturing, 2007)

Food products	£22,587,000
Paper products	£19,831,000
Chemical products	£19,508,000

Mining

Oil (2009–2010)	444,528,000 barrels
Sand and gravel (2009)	65,800,000 metric tons
Coal (2009–2010)	17,182,000 metric tons

The fishing industry has long been a major part of England's economy. Important catch includes cod, mackerel, haddock, and whiting.

Industry and Mining

The Industrial Revolution began in England, and manufacturing remains an important part of the economy. Major manufacturing industries include the production of food products, medicines and other chemicals, iron and steel, electronics, and textiles. The United Kingdom is one of the world's largest exporters of automobiles and has a thriving aerospace industry.

The most valuable mineral resource of the United Kingdom is oil, which lies under the North Sea. Coal has long been an important mineral resource in England, helping fuel the Industrial Revolution. Other important mining products today include tin, zinc, sand, gravel, limestone, dolomite, and clay. Gold and silver deposits are still the property of the royal family.

Services

Service industries make up by far the largest part of the English economy. About four out of every five working English people work in services. Service sector jobs include everything from real estate agent to doctor to teacher to car mechanic.

Banking and finance make up one of England's biggest service sectors. London is among the most powerful financial centers

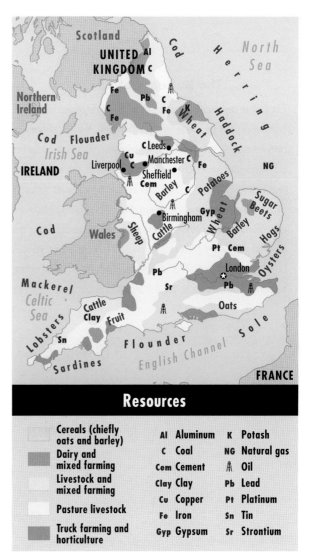

Resources

Cereals (chiefly oats and barley)	Al	Aluminum	K	Potash
Dairy and mixed farming	C	Coal	NG	Natural gas
Livestock and mixed farming	Cem	Cement	⚒	Oil
	Clay	Clay	Pb	Lead
Pasture livestock	Cu	Copper	Pt	Platinum
	Fe	Iron	Sn	Tin
Truck farming and horticulture	Gyp	Gypsum	Sr	Strontium

Fancy Wheels

Rolls-Royce has been making luxury cars in Manchester since 1904. Although Rolls-Royce is now owned by the German car company BMW, the cars are still built by hand in England. The new Ghost model costs about $250,000. The Phantom costs almost twice that much. A separate Rolls-Royce company headquartered in London is the world's second-largest maker of airplane engines.

The World of Work **73**

The Business of Chocolate

Chocolate arrived in England from the West Indies about 1650. At first it was sold as medicine, but then milk and sugar were added, and it became a hot chocolate drink. English chocolate has been an important product ever since. The first chocolate candy bar was made in Bristol in 1847. A couple of decades before that, in 1824, John Cadbury had opened a shop in Birmingham and sold chocolate drinks, coffee, and tea. In 1905, the Cadbury company created the Dairy Milk bar, a chocolate candy bar. More than a hundred years later it is still being sold. In 2010, Cadbury was bought by Kraft Foods, an American company.

in the world, and a hub of international business. More than five hundred banks have offices in London. Traditionally, the financial heart of England was an old part of central London called the City of London. Today, London's financial district has expanded to include part of the Docklands region, which was once part of the Port of London.

Money Facts

The main unit of English money is the pound sterling, which uses the symbol £. Each pound is divided into one hundred pence. Paper money comes in values of 5, 10, 20, and 50 pounds. Coins have values of 1, 2, 5, 10, 20, and 50 pence, as well as 1 and 2 pounds. All coins and bills have a profile of Queen Elizabeth II on the front. The back of each bill has an image of a significant figure from English history. For example, the 5-pound note depicts Elizabeth Fry, a prison reformer, and the 10-pound note shows naturalist Charles Darwin. All the coins except the 2-pound coin were redesigned in 2008. Matthew Dent, a young graphic designer, won a contest to create the new design. The back of each of the six redesigned coins shows part of the royal shield. Together, the six coins laid out in the correct arrangement form the entire shield. In 2012, US$1.00 equaled £0.65, and £1.00 equaled U.S. $1.54.

A New Economic Center

For hundreds of years, the Docklands was a thriving port where ships lined up to be loaded and unloaded. But in the 1960s, shipping companies began using huge cargo ships that required deep-water ports. The Docklands was no longer useful, and it was abandoned. The docks sat quiet, and poverty among nearby residents was high.

In the 1980s, the city began to redevelop the area. Starting with Canary Wharf, where Britain's tallest building is located, the Docklands has turned into a major financial center. Many commuters from the suburbs work in the Docklands rather than in the center of London. Construction of the Docklands Light Railway made getting to work there even easier. An urban airport, London City Airport, was also built in the area. The University of East London was formed out of several small technical colleges, attracting thousands of students to the Docklands.

East London has also become a center for technology and Internet companies. It's an especially good place for start-ups, which are new companies hoping to make it big. There are plenty of young, technically minded people to fill the jobs. Google, the huge Internet company, opened a big office there in 2012.

Tourists come from all over the world to visit England's historic sites. Every year, more than half a million people visit Warwick Castle, which was built in 1068.

Tourism is enormously important to the English economy. Tourists rent hotel rooms, eat in restaurants, and travel on trains and airplanes. London alone has about fifteen million international tourists every year, more than any other city in Europe. Top attractions in London include the British Museum, which displays art and artifacts from all around the world, and art museums such as the National Gallery and the Tate Modern. Elsewhere around the country, people visit to marvel at the mysteries of Stonehenge, explore dark castles, and walk along crumbling cliffs.

The London Eye

A great way to see London is from the London Eye, the largest Ferris wheel in Europe. It is located on the south bank of the River Thames across from the Houses of Parliament. It is one of the most popular tourist attractions in England. The wheel is 443 feet (135 m) tall. Around the edge of the wheel are thirty-two gondolas, which are completely enclosed and air-conditioned. The gondolas are so large that visitors can walk around them while admiring the astounding view during the half-hour ride.

Power

Coal supplied England's power needs for generations. But burning the coal to run machinery and heat homes sent huge billows of smoke into the air. Thick smog hung in the air all the time. The smog harmed the environment and people's health. Over time, British coal mining became outdated, and the coal became more expensive. Coal mining remained an

Let's Play

Merlin Entertainments Group, headquartered in Poole, England, is the world's second-largest amusement park company in the world, after Disney. It has Legoland parks in the United States. It also owns the Madame Tussauds wax museums around the world, the London Eye Ferris wheel, and Britain's largest theme park—Alton Towers. It even owns Warwick Castle, a thousand-year-old castle that was built on the orders of William the Conqueror.

important industry in the United Kingdom until the 1990s. But by 2005, the amount of coal mined there had been reduced by 90 percent.

England has had nuclear power since 1956, when the world's first commercial nuclear power plant began operating in Cumbria. Before the end of the century, nuclear reactors produced 26 percent of the electricity used in the United Kingdom. That percentage is now shrinking because the nation's use of natural gas is growing. England gets most of its gas from under the North Sea.

The United Kingdom is committed to generating electricity by renewable sources, such as wind power and solar power. The nation now has more than 3,500 wind turbines that produce electricity.

The British government has agreed to produce 15 percent of its energy needs from renewable sources by 2020. The nation

Capturing the Wind

In 2010, the world's largest offshore wind farm, the Thanet Offshore Wind Farm, began operation. More than 100 giant wind turbines are planted in the North Sea off Kent. As the turbines turn, they generate electricity. Underwater cables carry this electricity to land. Each turbine is 380 feet (116 m) high. Though they are located 7 miles (11 km) out at sea, they are so tall that they can be seen from shore. Twelve other smaller wind farms are also located around the British coastline, and throughout the United Kingdom today there are about 250 more operating wind farms.

In England, people drive on the left side of the road, whereas in the United States, Canada, and most of Europe people drive on the right side. Because driving on the left is unusual, some signs in England warn people which direction they need to look when crossing streets. Around the world, most of the countries that drive on the left are former British colonies. In England, people walking on sidewalks also stay to the left.

was well on its way by 2011, with 9.6 percent of all the electricity in the United Kingdom coming from renewable sources.

Transportation

England is a densely populated country, and people have many choices for how to travel. Roads crisscross the land. Today, more than two-thirds of UK households have at least one car.

London streets get congested with traffic.

Railways also spread out from London across the land. For a long time, English railways were cut off from continental Europe by the English Channel. Trains had to stop at the shore, and passengers had to board ferries to cross to France and the Netherlands. That changed in 1994 when the Channel Tunnel—often called the Chunnel—began to operate. One of the largest engineering projects ever, the tunnel runs for 31 miles (50 km) under the English Channel. Two rail lines carry cars, buses, freight, and passengers between Folkestone, England, and Calais, France.

A new system of trains called the Docklands Light Railway, or DLR, opened in 1987. It now carries more than

A train leaves the Channel Tunnel. About seventeen million passengers travel through the tunnel every year.

Crossrail is a new subway system being built underneath London. It is expected to begin running by 2018. It will have thirty-seven stations along a 13-mile (21 km) route. The Crossrail will weave between the tunnels of the old subway system and the basements of buildings. By the time it is ready, London will have an additional one million or more residents and will need the expanded transportation.

seventy million passengers a year, primarily to the Docklands area of London. It has forty-five stations on routes covering 19 miles (31 km). It is part of the Transport for London system, which includes buses, the London Underground (the subway system), and boats on the Thames.

Every major city in England has at least one airport. London has many more than that, but the five largest are Heathrow, Gatwick, Stansted, Luton, and London City (in the Docklands). Heathrow is the city's biggest airport and handles the most international passengers of any airport in the world. More than sixty-five million passengers travel through Heathrow each year, and it has no room to grow. An additional airport is being considered. It would be located on the Isle of Grain in the Thames Estuary, and would include a high-speed rail line going into the city and to the other airports.

The London Underground is the oldest subway system in the world. It began operating in 1863.

People and Language

IN 2011, HUMORIST AND AUTHOR JOE QUEENAN wrote in *Time* magazine: "I have been married to an Englishwoman for 34 years and find the folks from Blighty, at their best, to be tough, determined, resourceful, wickedly funny and much better cooks than they are given credit for."

"Blighty" has been a slang name for England since the nineteenth century when people in India used it. It derived from a word used in India to mean "province." English people and Americans may speak the same language, but their versions vary in many ways.

Opposite: **About 17.5 percent of the people in England are under age fifteen.**

The English Language

The English we speak and write today grew out of a mixture of many influences: German from tribal peoples, Norse from the Vikings, French from the Normans, and Latin from the Romans and the Catholic Church. In more recent years, words and phrases have entered the language via Hindi from India and American English from the United States. This variety of sources gives English the largest vocabulary of any language.

Old English

One of the oldest pieces of writing in England is *Beowulf*, a long epic poem about a hero who battles a monster called Grendel, but later dies from a wound inflicted by a dragon. It was written sometime between 600 and 900 CE in West Saxon, which is a dialect of Old English. There are many modern translations of the poem. In one version, the first lines are:

> So. The Spear-Danes in days gone by
> and the kings who ruled them had courage and
> greatness.
> We have heard of those princes' heroic campaigns.

Around 1417, King Henry V made English the official language of England by declaring that it should be used for official records. He was trying to get the support of common people at a time when the aristocrats were still speaking French and

In England, sweaters are called jumpers.

Translating English into English

Thousands of words that are common in England have to be "translated" for Americans. Here are a few.

British English	American English
biro	ballpoint pen
brilliant	fabulous, wonderful
candyfloss	cotton candy
chemist	drugstore
chips	French fries
crisps	potato chips
footie	soccer
fortnight	two weeks
gaol (same pronunciation)	jail
hols	holidays, especially from school
inverted commas	quotation marks
jumper	sweater
lift	elevator
lorry	truck
tosh	nonsense

the church was using Latin. He has been called the Father of Written English. Today, English is the most common language used around the world.

The language used in England and the language used in the United States are not exactly the same. For example, the vehicle Americans call trucks, English people call lorries. Words are also sometimes spelled differently. Words that end in -or in American English are generally spelled -our in British English. So *color* is spelled *colour*. Also, words that end in -er in the United States are usually spelled with -re in England. Thus, the English write *centre* rather than *center*.

Population of Major Cities (2010 est.)

City	Population
London	8,615,000
Birmingham	1,036,900
Liverpool	816,200
Leeds	810,200
Sheffield	640,720

Most people who live in the West London neighborhood of Southall are of South Asian descent.

Other Languages

As a result of immigration, people in England speak many different languages. There are at least one hundred different languages spoken in homes throughout London. Punjabi, a language spoken in India and Pakistan, is the second most used language in the country after English. Bengali is a language spoken in Bangladesh and India. The number of people in England who speak Bengali and a similar language called Sylheti is greater than the number who speak Punjabi.

Cantonese, a type of Chinese spoken by many Chinese immigrants, is also common. Arabic is becoming more common, especially in London. It is spoken by people from Egypt, Morocco, Lebanon, and other Middle Eastern countries.

Population

In 2011, the United Kingdom was home to about 62,698,000 people. About 52,234,000 of those people lived in England. If England were its own nation, it would be the twenty-fifth most populated nation in the world.

England's population is growing rapidly. Some experts say that by 2050 the United Kingdom will have 77,000,000 residents, making it the most populous nation in the European Union. It will have bypassed Germany and France.

England is also one of the most densely populated countries in Europe. In 2008, about 1,023 people lived in every square mile (395 per sq km) of England. The only nation in the European Union more densely populated is Malta, a small island near Sicily in the Mediterranean Sea.

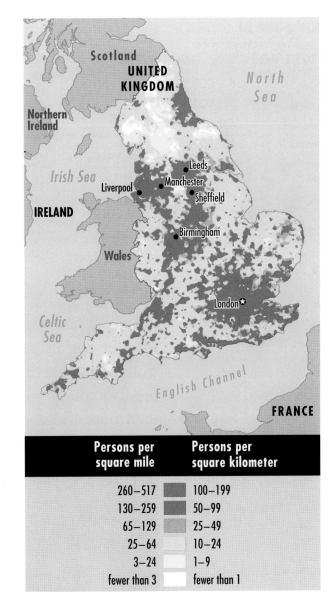

Persons per square mile		Persons per square kilometer
260–517		100–199
130–259		50–99
65–129		25–49
25–64		10–24
3–24		1–9
fewer than 3		fewer than 1

Birthplace of English Immigrants (2011 est.)

India	649,000
Poland	519,000
Pakistan	432,000
Ireland	332,000
Germany	265,000

Where They Come From

People from London are called Londoners, but the names for people from other places are not always so obvious. Here are some of the more unusual terms:

Blackpudlians	from Blackpool
Brummies	from Birmingham
Cornishman or Cornishwoman	from Cornwall
Geordies	from the Newcastle region
Liverpudlians	from Liverpool
Loiners	from Leeds
Mancunians	from Manchester
Salopians	from Shropshire
Tykes	from Yorkshire

Immigration

Most of England's population growth is from immigration. This means that the percentage of immigrants in the British population is growing. In 2001, 8.3 percent of the people in the United Kingdom were immigrants. By 2011, that number had grown to 12.1 percent.

People shopping at a Polish sausage stand in London. About 133,000 people born in Poland live in London.

Since 1990, citizens of any country within the European Union have the right to move into any other country within the EU. That has brought many immigrants to England from eastern European countries. An estimated 519,000 Poles now live in England.

Altogether, about one-third of immigrants to the UK come from European Union countries, while two-thirds come from other countries. In 2011, the largest number of immigrants—about 9.3 percent—came from India. Many also came from Pakistan, Poland, Bangladesh, and China.

Pakistanis are the third-largest immigrant group in England.

Ben Kingsley won the Academy Award for Best Actor for his portrayal of Mohandas Gandhi in the 1982 movie *Gandhi*.

Ethnic England (2009)

White	87.5%
South Asian	6.0%
Black	2.9%
Mixed race	1.9%
Chinese	0.8%
Other	0.8%

The English use the term *British Asian* to include Indians and Pakistanis, but not East Asians, who are from China or Indonesia. British Asians are concentrated in the borough called Tower Hamlets in London's East End, where the Docklands have been redeveloped. Tower Hamlets is about 30 percent Asian, whereas the whole of London is only about 13 percent Asian.

Many British Asians are world famous. World champion boxer Jawaid Khaliq is Pakistani, but he was born in Nottingham. Nasser Hussain, who was captain of the England cricket team, was born in India but raised in England. Novelist Salman Rushdie was born in India but moved to England to attend university and spent several decades there. Academy Award–winning actor Ben Kingsley was born Krishna Pandit Bhanji in North Yorkshire.

People perform a traditional dragon dance in London to celebrate Chinese New Year.

London and Liverpool have many East Asians, especially of Chinese descent. Chinese immigrants have been coming to England for two hundred years, and today England has a larger Chinese population than any other European country. *British Chinese* is the term used for the English-born Chinese. Many recent Chinese immigrants speak Cantonese. Many also speak English because they came from Hong Kong, an island off China that the British ruled for 156 years before transferring it back to Chinese control in 1997.

Immigrants from the islands in the Caribbean came to England in large numbers after World War II. The largest concentrations of people of Caribbean descent are in London and Birmingham.

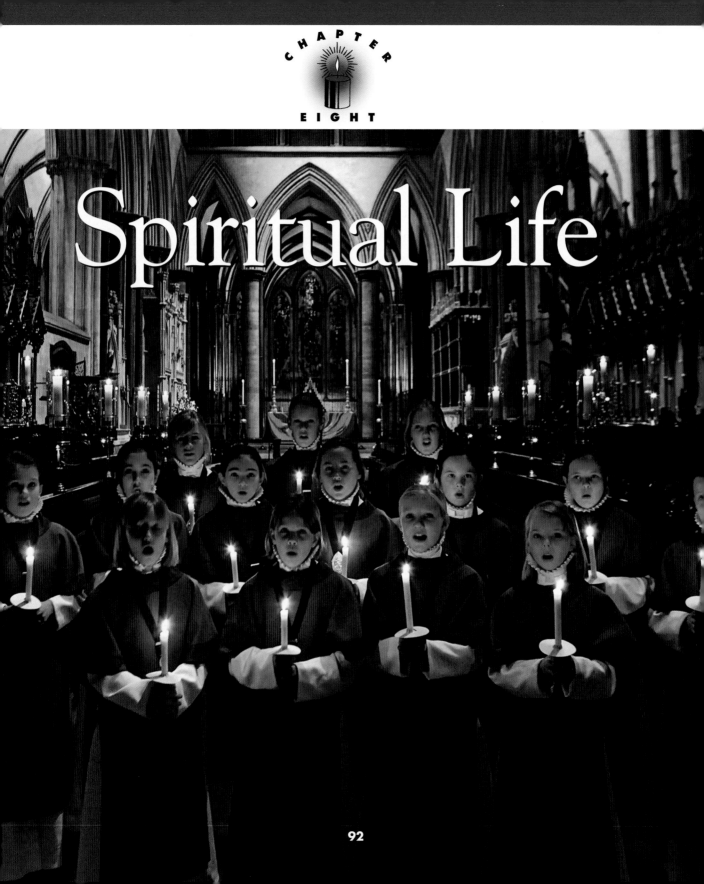

CHAPTER

EIGHT

Spiritual Life

ENGLAND'S NEWEST OFFICIALLY RECOGNIZED religion is also its oldest: Druidry. Druids were part of the culture of the ancient Celtic people who settled in Great Britain and Ireland. The Druids worshipped the earth and sun, nature, and the spirit in all things. Today, its few members—perhaps ten thousand—appear regularly in the news because of their events at Stonehenge. Many people think that Stonehenge was a Druid site, but it was actually built long before Druidry began.

Opposite: **Members of the children's choir sing in Salisbury Cathedral, which has been in use for more than 750 years.**

Early Christianity

The Anglo-Saxons practiced a religion with many gods. These gods were probably the ones worshipped by their ancestors in Germany. Among these gods were Woden and Thor. The Anglo-Saxon kings claimed to be descendants of such gods.

A few Anglo-Saxons converted to Christianity during Roman times. Several were martyrs, meaning they were killed for their beliefs. One martyr was Alban, who was beheaded

Mythical Creatures

The myths and tales from England are populated with such characters as elves, fairies, sprites, brownies, hobgoblins, imps, giants, and ghosts. These are the usually unseen creatures whose pranks and deeds explain the small mysteries of life, such as what was howling in the woods, why the milk spoiled so quickly, what caused the river to flood and spoil a crop, why a baby died, why the knitting yarn got all tangled. Most of these creatures come from the Germanic tales that traveled to England with the Angles and Saxons. Today, these creatures inhabit entertaining folktales.

around possibly 209 CE. He was later declared a saint, a person of exceptional holiness. St. Alban is considered the first British saint.

Christianity did not become common in England until years later. In about 580 CE, a king named Ethelbert, who ruled Kent, married a Christian woman named Bertha, who was from the continent. Though it is not known for sure, it is possible that Bertha encouraged the pope in Rome, the leader of the Christian Church, to send someone to England to spread Christianity. Pope Gregory I sent Augustine, a monk, in 597. Ethelbert promptly became a Christian. In those days, what the king did, the people did, too. Ethelbert's realm was now Christian.

Ethelbert provided the money to build a monastery for Augustine at the town of Canterbury. Augustine became the first Archbishop of Canterbury. Over the centuries, Canterbury

Pilgrims traveling to Canterbury

increased in size and magnificence. In *The Canterbury Tales*, written in the fourteenth century by Geoffrey Chaucer, pilgrims (travelers on a religious quest) tell tales to keep themselves entertained on the way to Canterbury.

The English Saint

Henry II appointed his friend Thomas Becket as Archbishop of Canterbury in 1162. Becket made decisions based on the idea of the church being superior to the king. This made Henry angry. The king wanted someone to get rid of Becket, and four of his knights murdered the archbishop in Canterbury Cathedral in 1170. Miracles were soon being attributed to Becket, and the pope declared him a saint.

England belonged to the Roman Catholic Church until the time of Henry VIII. In 1534, the king broke from Rome and declared that he, and not the pope, was head of the church in England. He broke up the monasteries, mainly to get hold of the vast amounts of land the church owned. He formed the Church of England, a Protestant church, which is still the established state church of England. It later became the Anglican Church, also known as the Episcopal Church. The Archbishop of Canterbury is head of the Church of England.

Rowan Williams became the Archbishop of Canterbury in 2003.

Christianity Today

The last time the British census collected information about religion was in 2001. At that time, almost 72 percent of the people said they were Christian. Of this group, 62 percent were Anglican. The next largest groups were Roman Catholic, Presbyterian, and Methodist.

Depending on how the question is asked, however, the number of British people who say they are Christian is much lower. The British Social Attitudes survey is taken every year. It asks people which religion they belong to. In 2011, 50 percent said none, and only 20 percent said Anglican. Rates of church attendance are lower still. Even among those who belong to a religion, 56 percent said they never attend church. Only 14 percent of church members attend services once a week.

Worshippers attend a service in Westminster Cathedral in London. It is the largest Catholic church in England.

King James Bible

The most famous book ever produced in London is the King James Version of the Bible. It was originally published in 1611. Seven years before, King James I brought together scholars to translate the Bible into English. It became the main English translation for four hundred years. Newer translations of the Bible are easier to understand, but many people still prefer the poetry of the King James Version.

Other Religions

Islam is the second most common religion in England. Followers of Islam are called Muslims. Muslims have lived in England for almost a thousand years. Chaucer mentioned Arabic scholars in *The Canterbury Tales*. When England controlled India through the East India Company, some Muslims who worked for the company moved to England. In recent decades, many Muslims have come to England from India, Pakistan, Bangladesh, and various African countries.

London, Bradford, and Birmingham have the largest Muslim populations in England. The East London Mosque and London Muslim Centre in the Tower Hamlets section of London is the heart of England's largest Muslim community. A third of the people in Tower Hamlets are Muslims of Bangladeshi descent. The area has at least forty mosques, Islamic houses of worship. The oldest mosque in England is the Shah Jahan Mosque, built in 1889 in Woking, near London.

England did not have large numbers of Buddhists until the twentieth century. Buddhism started in Asia. Unlike some other religions, Buddhism did not spread in England as a result of immigration. Instead, English people went to Asia to study Buddhism and then practiced it when they returned home. Most English Buddhists live in London, and most are white.

England has had Jewish residents since the time of the Norman Conquest. Jews were forced out of England in 1290, but some stayed and continued to practice their religion in secret. Gradually, Jewish communities grew. England saw a large influx of Jews in the early twentieth century, when many Russian Jews fled persecution.

England also has large communities of Hindus and Sikhs. Both of these religions began in India, and the number of followers grew over the course of the twentieth century as many Indians moved to England.

Religion in the United Kingdom (2001)

Christian	71.8%
Muslim	2.8%
Hindu	1%
Sikh	0.6%
Jewish	0.5%
Buddhist	0.3%
No religion/ did not answer	23%

Hindu women in Oxford carry pots during a Ghari Puja ceremony, which is held the night before a wedding.

Art and Sports

MUSIC HAS BEEN CENTRAL TO ENGLISH CULTURE for hundreds of years. King Henry VIII wrote popular songs, called madrigals, that the people in his court enjoyed. They are still played and sung today. Many other monarchs sponsored, or paid for the creation of, music. George Frideric Handel came to London from Germany to write music for the king. He wrote one of the most often sung choral works, *Messiah*, in London.

The London Symphony Orchestra played its first concert in 1904 and has been performing ever since. Since 1982 its home has been the Barbican Centre, located in the City of London.

Opposite: **The Beatles dominated the British music charts beginning with their first album, *Please Please Me* in 1963.**

Popular Music

English popular music has been a dominant force around the world since the 1960s, a period known as the British Invasion. The Beatles were the most popular band of the era. According

The Record Breaker

The *Guinness Book of Records* lists Paul McCartney, one of the members of the Beatles, as the "most successful musician and composer in popular music history." His song "Yesterday," which he wrote for the Beatles in 1965, has been recorded by more than 2,200 musicians, making it the most recorded song in history.

to some estimates, the Beatles have sold a billion records worldwide. The edgier Rolling Stones, with lead singer Mick Jagger, were also hugely popular.

The 1970s saw the rise of pop stars such as Elton John, who had huge hits with "Goodbye Yellow Brick Road" and "Rocket Man." John's success has continued through the decades. In

Elton John has sold more than 250 million records.

1997, he released a new recording of his hit song "Candle in the Wind," which was originally written and produced in 1973. The new recording became the biggest selling record of all time, with sales of thirty-three million copies worldwide. He has also written songs for popular shows such as *The Lion King*.

In the 1990s, bands such as Blur and Oasis hit the top of the charts. More recently, many female British singers, including Leona Lewis and Adele, have reached the top. Adele, whose full name is Adele Adkins, won six Grammy Awards in 2012 with her soulful singing and personal lyrics. Her album *21* has sold more than four million copies and is the biggest-selling album of the twenty-first century.

Adele won six Grammy Awards in 2012, including Album of the Year, for *21*, and Record of the Year, for the single "Rolling in the Deep."

Beatrix Potter published twenty-three children's books, beginning in 1902 with *The Tale of Peter Rabbit.*

Writers

English readers can start getting to know their country's writers in early childhood with the Peter Rabbit and Tom Kitten stories of Beatrix Potter. They can move on to Edith Nesbit's *The Railway Children*, then the Harry Potter books by J. K. Rowling. For horse lovers, there's Anna Sewell's *Black Beauty* or Enid Bagnold's *National Velvet.*

English writers have produced many great books for older readers as well. Jane Austen wrote novels that carefully detailed society and manners, such as *Pride and Prejudice*. Charles Dickens wrote stories mixing social criticism and comedy, which reveal the hardships of life in London in the 1800s. *Jane Eyre*, by Charlotte Brontë, and *Wuthering Heights*, by her sister, Emily Brontë, offer atmospheric romance. George Orwell's *1984* and *Animal Farm* provide sharp social commentary. H. G. Wells was one of the earliest science fiction writers. British writers invented the mystery novel, starting with *The Woman in White* by Wilkie Collins in 1859. They also invented fantasy, with *Alice's Adventures in Wonderland*, by Lewis Carroll, and *The Lord of the Rings* trilogy, by J. R. R. Tolkien.

Britain's Most Influential Woman

Who is the most influential woman in England? Is it the queen? No. According to a survey of magazine editors in 2010, the most influential British woman is J. K. Rowling, the author of the Harry Potter books about a lonely boy who learns he is a wizard. Rowling was born Joanne Rowling in Gloucestershire.

She began writing the books when she was unemployed, caring for her small daughter on her own, and living with the help of government assistance. The first Harry Potter book was published in 1997, and six more followed in the next ten years. The books became a phenomenon. Children lined up to buy each new book at the stroke of midnight when it first went on sale and then hungrily read it in a day. The books sold hundreds of millions of copies and were made into the most successful movie series in history. The books, the movies, and Harry Potter merchandise made Rowling a billionaire.

William Shakespeare, who wrote in the late 1500s and early 1600s, is generally considered the world's greatest playwright and the greatest English-language writer. He wrote historical plays about England's kings, such as *Henry V* and *Richard III*; comedies about romance gone awry, such as *A Midsummer Night's Dream*; and great tragic stories, such as *Hamlet* and *Romeo and Juliet*.

TV and Movies

The British Broadcasting Corporation (BBC) is the government-owned radio and television company in England. The world's longest-running TV show for children is the BBC's

Shakespeare's *Romeo and Juliet* (right) has been filmed many times. It was also adapted into the musical *West Side Story*.

Blue Peter. The show is named for the sailing flag that means the boat is ready to sail. Since its start in 1958, it has introduced children to activities, holidays, pets, and toys. The show has had many different hosts, or presenters, over its run of almost five thousand shows.

The premier school of acting in England is the Royal Academy of Dramatic Art, called RADA, which is located in London. It was founded in 1904 and is associated with King's College London. Its graduates include such legendary actors as John Gielgud, Anthony Hopkins, Kenneth Branagh, Ralph Fiennes, Helen Mirren, and Alan Rickman. Other prominent schools of acting include Guildhall School of Music and Drama and the Bristol Old Vic Theatre School.

Ralph Fiennes played Lord Voldemort in the Harry Potter movies. He is also a respected Shakespearean actor.

Matt Smith is the eleventh person to play the Doctor in the long-running television show *Doctor Who.*

Most of the actors in the Harry Potter movies—the most popular series in movie history—are English. Daniel Radcliffe, Emma Watson, and Rupert Grint, the three young stars of the series, grew up while making the eight films set at Hogwarts School of Witchcraft and Wizardry.

Many British TV shows have also been popular around the world. *Doctor Who* holds the record as the longest-running science fiction show ever. It first aired in 1963. The popular saga *Upstairs, Downstairs* aired in the 1970s. Set in the early twentieth century, it was about a wealthy family and the servants who worked for them. Recently, new episodes were released as a sequel to the original. *Downton Abbey,* which first aired in 2010, is also about a wealthy British family and their servants in the years before and during World War I. It is one of the most critically acclaimed shows on the air.

Reality shows are also popular in England. Simon Cowell, a Brighton native, is a music producer who has become a force in the television industry. He has been involved with the production of such hit shows as *American Idol*, *The X Factor* in both the United Kingdom and the United States, *Britain's Got Talent*, and *America's Got Talent*. He often finds talent on these shows for his recording company.

Simon Cowell is hugely successful as both a TV producer and a TV personality.

In England, wealthy aristocrats could afford to pay great painters to record their faces, their horses, their castles, and their children. Because of this, England has a great collection of art. Much of it is displayed at London's Tate Britain museum. Another branch of the Tate, called the Tate Modern, is located in a converted power plant in London. The Tate Modern displays one of the world's greatest collections of modern art and is the most visited modern art museum in the world.

J. M. W. Turner painted *The Fighting Téméraire* in 1934.

One of England's greatest painters, J. M. W. Turner, was a master landscapist. He is especially remembered for his dramatic watercolors and oil paintings of the sea. Since 1984, the Tate Britain has given a prize named in Turner's honor. The Turner Prize is presented only to artists under the age of fifty. It is now the best-known art prize in Britain.

In the late 1980s, a group called Young British Artists brought sensationalism into their creations, known as Britart. One of the best-known of this

Anish Kapoor (left) and Cecil Balmond (right) designed an observation tower called the ArcelorMittal Orbit for the 2012 Olympics. It is the largest piece of public art in Great Britain.

group is Damien Hirst. Death is a major theme in his work, and some of his art includes dead animals preserved in chemicals. One work displays a tiger shark that is 13 feet (4 m) long. Hirst won the Turner Prize in 1995. Another winner of the Turner Prize is Anish Kapoor, a sculptor who was born in India but has lived in England since he was in art school. Kapoor often makes large, curving shapes that give the impression of having motion and life.

Science

In the 1600s, Isaac Newton made astounding discoveries that laid the foundation for modern science. According to legend, he discovered the concept of gravity after watching an apple fall from a tree. Why, he wondered, does the apple fall downward? Newton, who was born in Lincolnshire in 1642, also

Stephen Hawking was a professor at Cambridge University from 1979 to 2009.

discovered that light is made of many different colors of light mixed together. Through his studies of how planets move, he came up with laws of motion for all objects. He has been called the most influential scientist who ever lived.

Other Englishmen who helped develop modern science include Charles Darwin, who devised the theory of evolution, and Michael Faraday, who worked in the fields of electricity and magnetism. Among the most famous English scientists today is Stephen Hawking, a physicist and cosmologist (a scientist who studies the universe). He was born in Oxford in

1942. Hawking has a disease that makes it impossible for him to walk or talk. He communicates entirely through computers. Hawking has written several best-selling books, including *A Brief History of Time* and *The Grand Design*, which explore the big questions of the universe.

Sports

The most popular sport in England is soccer, which the English call football. Every major city has a team that belongs to the Football Association. In addition, the association has more than forty thousand football clubs, with men, women, and children of all ages. The clubs are from counties, towns, schools, and community groups.

The most successful football team in England is Manchester United. England's national team, made up of the best players from many teams, won the World Cup in 1966. National

Web Man

London-born Tim Berners-Lee invented the World Wide Web—the "www" in Web site addresses. He was born in 1955. His parents were involved in the development of the first commercial computers in the 1950s, so he learned about them early. He was in his twenties when he experimented with sharing information using hypertext. That is the language that displays in immediately readable format what you see in a Web site, instead of it needing to be decoded. He says that he created the Web by putting other people's work together to make something new.

Manchester City fans cheer on their soccer team.

teams from all over the world compete in the World Cup, which is the world's premier soccer tournament.

Many children and adults play an informal variety of soccer called five-a-side. It has only four players on the field, plus a goalkeeper. The players decide the rules in advance, except when they're participating in futsal, a variety of the game sponsored by the Football Association.

One of the oldest team games in England is cricket, which probably started in the sixteenth century. Cricket is somewhat similar to baseball in that a ball is pitched to a batter, and players run. But unlike baseball, cricket games can last for days. A new, shorter version of cricket called Twenty20 was introduced in 2003 for games between county teams. Instead of taking days, a game of Twenty20 can finish in about two and a half hours.

Another popular sport in England is rugby, which is something like American football. In rugby, however, players cannot run with the ball as they do in American football. Another difference is that rugby players do not wear much protective gear. Hundreds of thousands of people in England play this bruising game.

England is home to Wimbledon, the world's premier tennis tournament. The last English person to win a Wimbledon championship was Virginia Wade, in 1977.

Around the World

Ellen MacArthur is a sailor who was born in Derbyshire. Although Derbyshire is not near the sea, MacArthur fell in love with sailing. She grew up to become a record breaker. In 2005, she made the fastest journey around the world, sailing alone. She beat the previous record by more than a day. The queen honored her achievement by making her a dame, the female equivalent of a knight. She is believed to be the youngest person ever to be honored in that way—she was only twenty-nine at the time.

Food and Fun

ENGLAND ONCE HAD THE REPUTATION FOR HAVING bad, bland food. Today, however, it is known for its great chefs and restaurants. Jamie Oliver had a cooking show on TV in 1999, when he was only twenty-four. Since then he's had other cooking shows and has written books and won awards. His recipes are pared down to only a few ingredients so that they are easy to cook. He also works on helping people improve their diets, by recommending that they eat fewer processed foods.

What Is English Food?

One of the most popular foods in England is fish and chips. The fish is battered and then deep-fried. *Chips* is the English term for French fries. Another famous English food is Yorkshire pudding. It is not a pudding as Americans know it. Instead, it is a thin batter of milk, flour, and eggs that is cooked in the drippings from a roast beef or lamb. It is often served before the main course of a meal.

Cheeses

Many different kinds of cheeses are made in England. Most are sold only locally. The most famous English cheese is cheddar, created originally near Cheddar Gorge in Somerset. Others are Wensleydale, from North Yorkshire; Stilton (right), a soft, strong blue cheese originally from Cambridgeshire; and crumbly Cheshire, England's oldest cheese, which has been made for hundreds of years.

Drinking tea is a way of life in England. English people usually drink black tea with milk. It is common for people to drink several cups of tea over the course of the day.

As immigrants have come to England from all over the world, English food has changed. Indian and Chinese dishes are now common foods in England. There are an estimated ten thousand Indian restaurants in Great Britain. Many of them are run by people of Bangladeshi or Pakistani origin. Indian food is often flavored with a mix of spices called curry. These dishes are typically served with rice or flatbread. Chinese food is also hugely popular in England. Almost every community

Make It Yourself

A favorite food of many English kids is baked beans on toast. It might sound strange, but give it a try. It's a nutritious meal eaten for breakfast, lunch, or dinner.

To make this simple recipe, open a can of baked beans. Pour them into a saucepan and heat them on the stove until they are hot. In the meantime, make toast—one piece or two, depending on how hungry you are—using any kind of bread you like. Place the toast on a big plate. Spoon the hot baked beans over it. Eat and enjoy.

The British drink 165 million cups of tea every day.

has a Chinese take-out restaurant. In England "take-out" is called takeaway.

Education

Since 1870, children have been required to start school at age five, though many start at age four. Primary school goes until age eleven and secondary school lasts at least until age

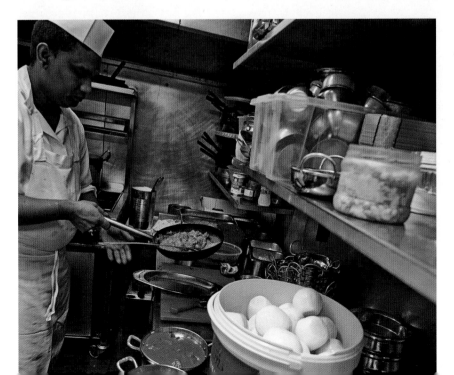

A chef prepares a curry at a restaurant in London. Indian restaurants are common throughout England.

sixteen. For decades, students could not leave school until age sixteen, though most went on until eighteen. Recently, the law was changed, requiring students to stay in school until age seventeen. Starting in 2015, all children will be required to attend school until age eighteen.

Most children go to state-run schools. England also has many private schools, called independent schools. One independent school is The King's School in Canterbury. It is believed to be the oldest school in England, dating back to 597.

Schoolchildren in London work on a science project.

About 7 percent of children attend private schools during the early years, and almost 20 percent of students ages sixteen to eighteen attend private schools. Most are day schools, but some are boarding schools, where students live, going home only on weekends or for the holidays.

To graduate from school, students take a series of exams called A Levels. These exams qualify them to go to college or university. The two oldest universities in England are Oxford (founded in 1214) and Cambridge (founded in 1284). Higher education used to be the privilege of only a few, but now many students attend college. There are many newer universities today, and more opportunities for young people to get college degrees. In 2009, an estimated 1.4 million students were in higher education in the United Kingdom. That's almost three times as many as twenty years earlier.

Students bicycle past the University of Cambridge. It is often ranked as the best university in the world.

Conkers

British children have been playing conkers for centuries. Conkers are the seeds in the green prickly fruit of the horse chestnut tree. In autumn the fruit falls from the trees and splits open, revealing the conkers.

To play the game, players choose a good, hard conker. Roald Dahl, the author of many classic children's books such as *Charlie and the Chocolate Factory* and *James and the Giant Peach*, wrote about conkers in his autobiography: "A great conker is one that has been stored in a dry place for at least a year," he wrote. "This matures it and makes it rock hard and therefore formidable [intimidating]." The device used in the game is made by hammering a nail through the center of a hard conker and putting a strong string, such as a shoelace, through the hole. The string is about 10 inches (25 cm) long and is knotted on one end to keep it from coming out of the hole.

Conkers requires two players. One player lets her conker dangle, holding it still, while the other player tries to hit it with his conker. He can swing it or use the string like a slingshot. If he misses, he gets another turn. Actually, players can make up their own rules. The game ends when one player has broken the other's conker.

A few years ago, students had to pay only small fees to attend universities, because the government funded the schools. But in recent years, the government has increased fees dramatically. The country was shocked in 2010 when students rioted in the streets. They were protesting cuts in educational funding and an increase in university tuition.

In 2010, students took to the streets to protest a plan to triple the cost of college tuition.

A Piece of the Past

Thatched cottages date back to before the Middle Ages. Thatching is roofing made from bundles of dried reeds or straw. Over the generations, people stopped using thatching and instead used tile or slate roofs. But now some wealthy people are enjoying thatched roofs once again. They have replaced their contemporary roofs with thatching, so their house has a historic and rustic look.

Life at Home

In cities, many people live in large apartment buildings, which in England are often called blocks of flats. Stores are usually located close by the apartments. Since the 1970s, people without much income have been provided public housing, usually in big apartment buildings called council housing because the town council manages them. Recently, the people who live in what is called social housing have been allowed to buy their flats if they want to.

Shoppers stroll along the high street in Glastonbury.

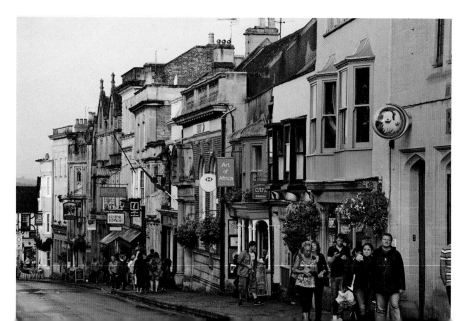

Outside cities, people generally live in houses in villages or small towns. There are two main kinds of villages. One has the houses built along the main street. If stores line the main street, it is called the high street. Sometimes the houses are built right up to the sidewalk. Gardens are in the back and can't be seen. In the second kind of village, houses are built around a pond or a central grassy area, called the green. Sometimes, an ancient church sits in the middle of the green, which is often on the highest spot in town.

Holidays

"Remember, remember the fifth of November": These words refer to the events that are commemorated on Guy Fawkes Night. In 1605, Guy Fawkes and his Catholic friends plotted to blow up Parliament and the Protestant king, James I, in what is known as the Gunpowder Plot. Fawkes was arrested on November 5 while guarding the explosives. The people

Men's Dress

The suit that is now worn by men around the world was a British creation in the early 1800s. Before that, men wore fancy silk embroidered jackets over tights or knee breeches. Gradually, this style of clothes changed to matching pants and jackets. The shirt and tie combination is believed to have been introduced in the early 1800s by a "dandy" named Beau Brummell (left). The suits worn today were originally called lounge suits. Today, England is a fairly casual place. Most men wear jeans and T-shirts when not at work.

Dancers and floats fill the streets at the Notting Hill Carnival.

of London lit bonfires in thanks for the plot being thwarted. Today, the holiday is celebrated with bonfires and fireworks. Children sometimes make figures called Guys, by filling male clothing with stuffing. The Guys are burned in the bonfire. In recent years, Guy Fawkes celebrations have become less common. Instead, English people are celebrating Halloween, which comes just a few days earlier.

The large number of Indians who have moved to England in recent decades have brought with them some traditional holidays. Many cities now celebrate Diwali, the Hindu festival of lights, between mid-October and mid-November. People light small lamps made of clay to celebrate the conquest of good over evil. Firecrackers are lit to drive away evil.

For Muslims, the holiest time of year is Ramadan, a month in which they do not eat during the daylight hours. It is intended to teach people about patience and make them focus more on their spiritual life. The end of Ramadan is marked by a great feast called 'Id al-Fitr.

Notting Hill Carnival is the biggest party in England. Held for two days in August, it was started in 1964 by people who moved to London from the Caribbean after World War II. The carnival attracts more than a million people from all backgrounds who come together to enjoy the party.

English Holidays

New Year's Day	January 1
Good Friday	March or April
Easter Monday	March or April
St. George's Day	April 23
May Day	First Monday in May
Spring Bank Holiday	Last Monday in May
Summer Bank Holiday	Last Monday in August
Christmas Day	December 25
Boxing Day	December 26

Timeline

English History

Celts begin to arrive in England.	600–700 BCE
Romans cross the English Channel.	55–54 BCE
England becomes a Roman province.	43 CE
The Romans build Hadrian's Wall in northern England.	ca. 122
Anglo-Saxon tribes begin arriving in England.	ca. 450
The Anglo-Saxons convert to Christianity.	597
Norsemen (Vikings) take over English land.	867–897
The Normans invade England.	1066
Thomas Becket is murdered in Canterbury Cathedral.	1170
King John seals the Magna Carta.	1215
The Hundred Years' War is fought between England and France.	1337–1453
The Black Death kills half of England's population.	1348–1350
Henry VIII breaks with the Roman Catholic Church.	1534
Wales is annexed by order of Parliament.	1536
English ships destroy the Spanish Armada.	1588
The Great Fire destroys four-fifths of London.	1666

World History

ca. 2500 BCE	Egyptians build the pyramids and the Sphinx in Giza.
ca. 563 BCE	The Buddha is born in India.
313 CE	The Roman emperor Constantine legalizes Christianity.
610	The Prophet Muhammad begins preaching a new religion called Islam.
1054	The Eastern (Orthodox) and Western (Roman Catholic) Churches break apart.
1095	The Crusades begin.
1215	King John seals the Magna Carta.
1300s	The Renaissance begins in Italy.
1347	The plague sweeps through Europe.
1453	Ottoman Turks capture Constantinople, conquering the Byzantine Empire.
1492	Columbus arrives in North America.
1500s	Reformers break away from the Catholic Church, and Protestantism is born.

English History

England and Scotland are united.	1707
The Industrial Revolution begins in England.	ca. 1750
The American colonies declare independence from Great Britain.	1776
Great Britain and Ireland are united.	1801
The Irish Free State (now the Republic of Ireland) wins independence from the United Kingdom.	1921
German forces bomb the UK in the Battle of Britain	1940
India becomes independent of British rule.	1947
Margaret Thatcher becomes Britain's first female prime minister.	1979
Parliament passes the new House of Lords Act.	1999
Bombs explode on the London transport network, killing fifty-six people.	2005
The Olympic Summer Games are held in London.	2012

World History

1776	The U.S. Declaration of Independence is signed.
1789	The French Revolution begins.
1865	The American Civil War ends.
1879	The first practical lightbulb is invented.
1914	World War I begins.
1917	The Bolshevik Revolution brings communism to Russia.
1929	A worldwide economic depression begins.
1939	World War II begins.
1945	World War II ends.
1957	The Vietnam War begins.
1969	Humans land on the Moon.
1975	The Vietnam War ends.
1989	The Berlin Wall is torn down as communism crumbles in Eastern Europe.
1991	The Soviet Union breaks into separate states.
2001	Terrorists attack the World Trade Center in New York City and the Pentagon near Washington, D.C.
2004	A tsunami in the Indian Ocean destroys coastlines in Africa, India, and Southeast Asia.
2008	The United States elects its first African American president.

Fast Facts

Official name: United Kingdom of Great Britain and Northern Ireland

Official language: None

London

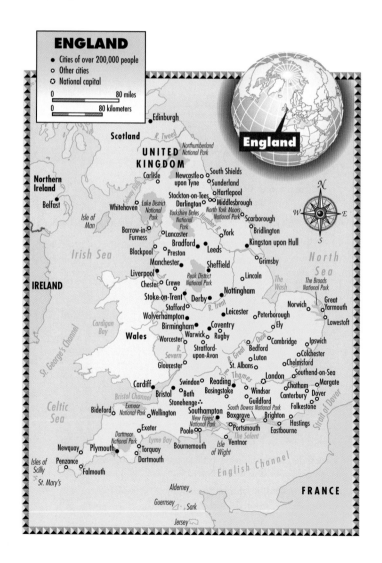

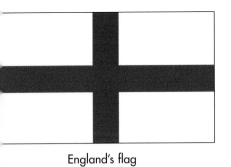

England's flag

Official religion:	Church of England
National anthem:	"God Save the Queen"
Type of government:	Constitutional monarchy and parliamentary democracy
Head of state:	Monarch
Head of government:	Prime minister
Area of country:	50,346 square miles (130,396 sq km)
Bordering countries:	Scotland to the north and Wales to the west
Highest elevation:	Scafell Pike, 3,210 feet (978 m) above sea level
Lowest elevation:	Usually sea level, but during low tide near Ely in Cambridgeshire, a small section of exposed land is about 15 feet (5 m) below sea level
Average high temperature:	In London, 74°F (23°C) in July; 47°F (8°C) in January
Average low temperature:	In London, 57°F (14°C) in July; 36°F (2°C) in January

Average annual rainfall:

East coast	20 inches (51 cm)
Western and northern hills	40 inches (102 cm)
Lake District	130 inches (330 cm)

National population (2011 est.):	England: 52,234,000; United Kingdom: 62,698,000

Dartmoor

Stonehenge

Population of major cities (2010 est.):

London	8,615,000
Birmingham	1,036,900
Liverpool	816,200
Leeds	810,200
Sheffield	640,720

Landmarks:

▶ *Canterbury Cathedral,* Canterbury

▶ *London Eye,* London

▶ *Stonehenge,* Salisbury

▶ *Tower of London,* London

▶ *Westminster Abbey,* London

▶ *Windsor Castle,* Berkshire

Economy: Services make up the largest part of the English economy. London is a global center of finance and England is a top tourist destination. Major manufacturing industries include food products, paper products, iron and steel, electronics, and textiles. The United Kingdom as a whole is one of the world's largest exporters of automobiles and has a thriving aerospace industry. The most valuable mineral resource of the United Kingdom is oil, which lies under the North Sea. Other important mining products include sand, gravel, coal, limestone, and clay. England's chief crops are wheat, barley, potatoes, sugar beets, and rapeseed oil.

Currency

Currency: The pound sterling. In 2012, US$1.00 = £0.65; £1.00 = U.S. $1.54

System of weights and measures: Metric system

Literacy rate: 100%

Schoolchildren

J. K. Rowling

Common English terms:

chemist	drugstore
chips	French fries
crisps	potato chips
gaol	jail
jumper	sweater
lift	elevator
lorry	truck
tosh	nonsense

Prominent English people:

Jane Austen (1775–1817)
Author

Charles Darwin (1809–1882)
Scientist

Charles Dickens (1812–1870)
Author

Elizabeth II (1926–)
Queen

Henry VIII (1491–1547)
King

Paul McCartney (1942–)
Musician and composer

Isaac Newton (1642–1727)
Founder of modern physics

J. K. Rowling (1965–)
Author

William Shakespeare (1564–1616)
Playwright and poet

To Find Out More

Books

▶ Berk, Ari. *William Shakespeare: His Life and Times*. Somerville, MA: Candlewick Press, 2010.

▶ Gravett, Christopher. *Knight: Noble Warrior of England 1200–1600*. New York: Osprey Publishing, 2008.

▶ Reeves, James. *Stories from England*. New York: Oxford University Press, 2009.

Music

▶ The Beatles. *The Beatles 1*. Capitol Records, 2000.

▶ *English Madrigals and Songs*. Naxos, 1996.

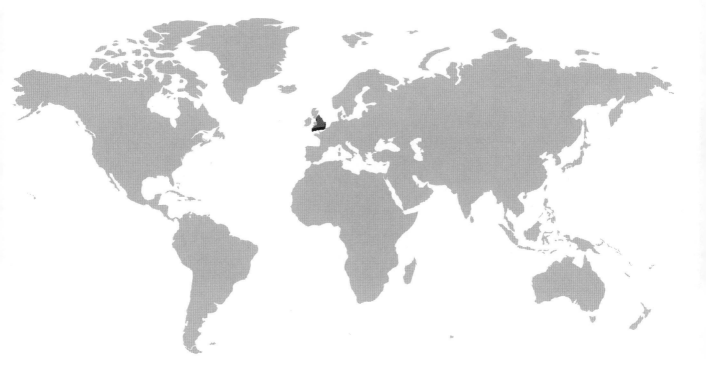

▶ Visit this Scholastic Web site for more information on England:
www.factsfornow.scholastic.com

Enter the keyword **England**

Index

Page numbers in *italics* indicate illustrations.

A

Act of Settlement, 61
Acts of Union, 45
agriculture
    crops, 71, 72
    early settlers and, 35
    economy and, 71, 72
    Fen Country, 20
    hedgerows, 31
    land area, *70*
    Wiltshire County, *70*
airports, 75, 81
Alban (saint), 93–94
A Level exams, 121
Alfred the Great, 40–41
Alton Towers, 77, *77*
American English language, 83, 85
Angle people, 36, 39, 40, 93, 94
Anglican Church, 96, 97
Anglo-Irish Treaty, 45
Anglo-Saxon people, 40, 93–94
animal life
    badgers, 29
    birds, 30–32
    cave lions, 27–28
    English robin (national bird), 31
    fallow deer, 29
    foxes, 29, *29*
    harvest mice, 29
    hedgehogs, 31, *31*
    hippopotamuses, 28
    livestock, 71
    otters, 29
    ponies, 29–30, *30*
    prehistoric, 20, *20*, 27–28

red deer, 28–29, *28*
Sites of Special Scientific Interest (SSSIs), 33
woolly mammoths, 28
Aquae Sulis, 38
Arabic language, 87
archaeology, 35, 38
Archbishops of Canterbury, 94, 95, 96, *96*
aristocracy, 41–42
Arkwright, Richard, 52
art, *11*, 21, *21*, 110–111, *110*, *111*
Arthur, king of England, 40, *40*
artifacts, 38
Astor, Nancy, 62, *62*
Astor, Waldorf, 62
Athelstan, king of Wessex and Mercia, 41
Augustine, Archbishop of Canterbury, 94
Austen, Jane, 104–105, 133
Australia, 19, 48

B

badgers, 29
Bagnold, Enid, 104
baked beans on toast, 118
Balmond, Cecil, *111*
Bangladesh, 56, 86, 88, 98, 118
Barbican Centre, 101
barrows, 35
Bath, 38, *38*
Battersea Shield, *34*
Battle of Britain, 55
Battle of Hastings, 41
Beaker People, 35
Beatles (musical group), *100*, 101–102
Becket, Thomas, Archbishop of Canterbury, 95
Bengali language, 86
Beowulf (epic poem), 84, *84*
Berkshire County, 60
Berners-Lee, Tim, 113, *113*
Bible, 98, *98*
Big Ben, 62, *62*
birds, 30–32
Birmingham, 25, 86, 91, 98
Black Death, 44, *44*

Blue Peter television show, 106–107
Blur (musical group), 103
Bodmin Moor, 22
Boudicca (Iceni leader), 38, *39*
Bradford, 98
Bristol, 74
Bristol Old Vic Theatre School, 107
Britannia (Roman goddess), 11, *11*
Britart, 110–111
British Broadcasting Corporation (BBC), 106–107
British Invasion, 101
British Isles, 11, 23
British Museum, 76
British Social Attitudes survey, 97
Brogdale, 24
Brontë, Charlotte, 105
Brontë, Emily, 105
Brummell, Beau, 125, *125*
Brunel, Isambard Kingdom, 53
Buckingham Palace, 60, *61*
Buddhism, 99

C

cabinet ministers, 63
Cabot, John, 44
Cabot, Sebastian, 44
Cadbury company, 74, *74*
Cambridgeshire County, 16
Cambridge University, *112*, 121, *121*
Cameron, David, *63*
Canary Wharf, 75
Canterbury, 94–95, *95*, 120
Canterbury Cathedral, 95
Canterbury Tales, The, (Geoffrey Chaucer), 95, 98
Cantonese language, 87, 91
Caribbean Islands, 91
Carnival holiday, *126*, 127
Carroll, Lewis, 105
cave lions, 27–28
Celtic people, 36, 37, 38, 93
chalk, 21–22, *21*
Channel Tunnel, 80, *80*
Charles I, king of England, 46
Charles, prince of Wales, 60
Chaucer, Geoffrey, 95, 98
cheese, 118, *118*

Cheshire County, 33
Chichester Harbour, 33
children, *82, 84, 92, 116*, 120, *120*, 122, *122*
China, 89, 90, 91, *91*, 118–119
Chinese New Year, *91*
chocolate, 74, *74*
Church of England, 44, 46, 62, 96
cities. *See also* towns; villages.
    Birmingham, 25, 86, 91, 98
    Bradford, 98
    Bristol, 74
    Canterbury, 94–95, *95*, 120
    Ely, 16
    Folkestone, 80
    Heathrow, 81
    Leeds, 25, 86
    Liverpool, *11*, 19, 25, *25*, 86, 91
    London, 13, 16, 24, *24*, 25, 34, *39,*
        42, 47, *47,* 53, 55, *55,* 57, *57,* 60,
        61, 62, *62,* 66–67, *66,* 73, 74,
        75–76, *77, 79,* 81, 86, *86,* 88, *88,*
        90, 91, *91,* 98, 99, 101, 105, 110
    Manchester, *52*
    Portsmouth, 24
    Sheffield, 25, *25,* 86
climate, 16, 23–24, *23, 24*
clothing, *84,* 125, *125*
coal, 72, 73, 77–78
coastline, *14,* 17–20, *17, 18*
Collins, Wilkie, 105
colonies, 48–49, *48,* 56, 79, 91
conkers (game), 122, *122*
Conservative Party, 64
Cornwall County, 18, 19, 27, 29, 35
Cotswolds, 33, *33*
cotton industry, 52, *52*
council housing, 124
Council of the European Union, 68–69
counties
    Berkshire, 60
    Cambridgeshire, 16
    Cheshire, 33
    Cornwall, 18, 19, 27, 29, 35
    Cumbria, 78
    Devon, 18, 22, *22,* 27
    Dorset, 27
    East Riding, 13

Kent, 18
Lincolnshire, 33, 111
map, *13*
names of, 12
Norfolk, 33, 38
North Riding, 13
Rutland, 13
Somerset, 38
Staffordshire, 23
Suffolk, 28
Sussex, 18
West Riding, 13
Wiltshire, *70*
Yorkshire, *12,* 13, 22, 25
Court of Appeal, 68, 69
Cowell, Simon, 108–109, *109*
cricket (sport), 90, 115
Cromwell, Oliver, 46–47, *46*
Crossrail subway system, 81
Crown Court, 68, 69
Cumbria County, 78
Cumbrian Mountains, 15
currency (pound sterling), 11, 56, 74, *74*
curry, 118, *119*

D
Dahl, Roald, 122
dance, *91, 126*
Danelaw religion, 40
Darby, Abraham, I, *50,* 51
Darby, Abraham, III, *50*
Dartmoor, *22, 22,* 29, 30
Darwin, Charles, 74, 112, 133
Dent, Matthew, 74
Devon County, 18, 22, *22,* 27
Dickens, Charles, 105, 133
Diwali festival, 127
Docklands Light Railway (DLR), 75,
    80–81
Docklands region, 75, *75,* 80–81, 90
Dorset County, 27
dragons, 60, *84, 91*
Drake, Francis, 45
Druids, 93

E
East End (London), 57, 90
East India Company, 48, 98

East London Mosque, 98
East Midlands region, 13
East of England region, 13
East Riding County, 13
economy
    agriculture and, 71, 72
    currency (pound sterling), 11, 56,
        74, *74*
    European Union (EU), 69
    exports, 72
    finance industry, 73–74, 75
    fishing industry, 72
    government and, 57
    Industrial Revolution, 50–53, *51,*
        71, 72, 73
    manufacturing, 51, 52, *52,* 72–73
    mining, 35, 72, 73, 77–78
    oil industry, 72, 73
    service industries, 20, 73–76
    tourism, 20, 76, *76,* 77
    trade, 35, 48
    World War II and, 55
education, 64, 65, *116,* 119–121, *120,*
    121, 123, *123*
electricity, 64, 78–79, *78,* 112
Elizabeth I, queen of England, 45
Elizabeth II, queen of England, 47, *58,*
    60, 74, *74,* 133
Ely, 16
English Channel, 17, 19, 80
English Civil War, 46, *46*
English language, 83–85, *84,* 91, 98
English robin (national bird), 31
Ethelbert, king of Kent, 94
European Commission, 69
European Parliament, 68, 69
European Union (EU), 56, 67, 68–69,
    87, 89
executive branch of government, 59,
    63–64, *63, 64,* 69
Exmoor, 22, 29, 30, *30*
exploration, 44, 45, 48, 49
exports, 72

F
fallow deer, 29
Faraday, Michael, 112
Fawkes, Guy, 125

Fen Country, 20
Fiennes, Ralph, 107, *107*
film industry, 90, 91, 106–108, *106, 107*
finance industry, 73–74, 75
fish and chips, 117
fishing industry, 72
five-a-side football, 114
Flash, 23
floodgates, 19, *19*
Folkestone, 80
folktales, 94
foods, 71, 72, 74, *74*, 117–119, *118, 119*
football, 113–114, *114, 116*
forests, 32, *32*
fossils, 20, *20*
foxes, 29, *29*
France, 17, 40, 41, 54, 80, 87

G
Geoffrey of Monmouth, 9, 40
geography
    beaches, 18, *18*
    chalk, 21–22, *21*
    coastline, *14*, 17–20, *17, 18, 26, 27*
    Cumbrian Mountains, 15
    elevation, 15, 16
    English Channel, 17, 19, 80
    estuaries, 19
    Fen Country, 20
    islands, 11, *14*, 16, 20, 37, 81, 87
    Jurassic Coast, 20, *20*
    lakes, 15, 16, 17, 33, *33*
    land area, 15, 16
    moors, 15, 22, *22*, 31, 32
    Needles, 20
    Pennine Mountains, 15, 33
    rivers, 8, 16, 19, *19*, 22, 25, *25, 35*, 52, 77, 81
    Scafell Pike, 15, 16
George I, king of England, 47
George III, king of England, 49
George, patron saint of England, 60
Germany, 39, 47, 54, 55, 73, 87, 88, 93, 101
Glorious Revolution, 47
"God Save the Queen" (national anthem), 68
government. *See also* monarchs.

cabinet ministers, 63
Council of the European Union, 68–69
Court of Appeal, 68, 69
Crown Court, 68, 69
economy and, 57
education and, 120, 123
elections, 59, 63, 64, 65
European Commission, 69
European Parliament, 68
European Union (EU), 68–69
executive branch, 59, 63–64, *63, 64*, 69
High Court, 68, 69
House of Commons, 49, 62, 63, 64, 69
House of Lords, 49, 62, 69
judicial branch, 65, 67–68, 69
legislative branch, 45, 46, 47, 59, 61–63, 68, 69, 125
local governments, 65
Magistrates' Court, 67–68, 69
Magna Carta, 43, *43*
Members of Parliament (MPs), 59, 62, 63, 64
military, 46, *46*, 49, 54, *54*
national parks and, 17, 25, 33
no-confidence votes, 64
Parliament, 45, 46, 47, 59, 61–63, *63*, 64, 65, 67, 69, 125
political parties, 64
prime ministers, 59, 63–64, *63, 64*, 69
protests, 57, 123, *123*
renewable energy and, 78, *78*
Supreme Court, 65, 67, 68
unitary authorities, 65
United Kingdom, 61
Great Britain, 9–10, 11, 15, 45, 93
Great Fire of London, 47, *47*
Great Western steamship, 53
greens, 125
Gregory I (pope), 94
Grint, Rupert, 108
Guildhall School of Music and Drama, 107
Gulf Stream, 23–24
Gunpowder Plot, 125

Guy Fawkes Night, 125–127
H
Hadrian's Wall, 33
Halloween, 127
Handel, George Frideric, 101
Harold II, king of England, 41
Harry Potter series, 104, 105, *107*, 108
harvest mice, 29
Hawking, Stephen, 112–113, *112*
Heathrow, 81
heaths, 32
hedgehogs, 31, *31*
hedgerows, 31
Henry II, king of England, 95
Henry V, king of England, 84–85, 106
Henry VI, king of England, 43
Henry VII, king of England, 44, 45
Henry VIII, king of England, 44, 45, *45*, 96, 101, 133
High Court, 68, 69
high streets, *124*, 125
Hinduism, 99, *99*
hippopotamuses, 28
Hirst, Damien, 111
historical maps. *See also* maps.
    British Empire, 1919, *49*
    Invaders and Settlers, *41*
    Roman Conquest of Britain, *37*
holidays
    national, 125–127
    religious, 127
Hong Kong, 91
House of Commons, 49, 62, 63, 64, 69
House of Lords, 49, 62, 69
Houses of Parliament, 62, 77
Humber River, 19
Hyde Park, 66, 67

I
Iceni people, 38, 39
'Id al-Fitr holiday, 127
immigration, 56, *56*, 86, *86*, 88–91, *88, 89, 118*
independent schools, 120
India, 48, *48*, 56, 83, 86, 88, 89, 90, 98, 118, 127
Indonesia, 90

Industrial Revolution, 50–53, *51*, 71, 72, 73
Ireland, 10, 11, 45, 54, 60, 93
Irish Sea, 17
iron, 36, *50*, 51, 72
Iron Age, 36
Islamic religion, 57, 98, 99, 127
Isle of Grain, 81
Isle of Wight, *14*, 16, 20
Isles of Scilly, 20

J
Jamaica, 56, *56*
James I, king of England, 45, 98, 125
James II, king of England, 47
John, Elton, 102–103, *102*
John, king of England, 43, *43*
Judaism, 99
judicial branch of government, 65, 67–68, 69
Jurassic Coast, 20, *20*
Jute people, 39

K
Kapoor, Anish, 111, *111*
Kent County, 18
King's College London, 107
Kingsley, Ben, *90*, 91
King's School, 120
kings. *See* monarchs.

L
Lake District, 15, 16, 17, 24, 33, *33*
Lake District National Park, 17, 33, *33*
Langhorne, Nancy, *See* Astor, Nancy.
languages, 36, 39, 40, 66, 83–85, *84*, 86–87, 98
Latin language, 39, 83, 85
Leeds, 25, 86
legislative branch of government, 45, 46, 47, 59, 61–63, 68, 69, 125
Lincolnshire County, 33, 111
literature, 9, 31, 40, 84, 90–91, 95, 104–106, 122, 133, *133*
Liverpool, *11*, 19, 25, *25*, 86, 91
livestock, 71
local governments, 65

London, 13, 16, 24, *24*, 25, *34*, 39, *42*, 47, *47*, 53, 55, *55*, 57, *57*, 60, *61*, 62, *62*, 66–67, 66, 67, 73, 74, 75–76, *77*, 79, 81, 86, *86*, 88, *88*, 90, 91, *91*, 98, 99, 101, 105, 110
London Bridge Tower. *See* Shard London Bridge.
London City Airport, 75
London Eye, *77*, 77
London Muslim Centre, 98
London Symphony Orchestra, 101
London Underground, 81, *81*

M
MacArthur, Dame Ellen, 115, *115*
Madame Tussauds wax museum, 77
Magistrates' Court, 67–68, 69
Magna Carta, 43, *43*
Major Oak, 32, *32*
Manchester, *52*, 73, 113, *114*
Manchester City football club, *114*
Manchester United football club, 113
manufacturing, 51, 52, *52*, 72–73
maps. *See also* historical maps.
    geopolitical, *10*
    London, 67
    population density, 87
    regions and counties, *13*
    resources, *73*
    topographical, *16*
marine life, 18, 21, 29
Mary, queen of England, 47
McCartney, Paul, *102*, *102*, 133
Members of Parliament (MPs), 59, 62, 63, 64
Merlin Entertainments Group, 77, *77*
Mersey Estuary, 25
Mersey River, 19
Messiah (George Frideric Handel), 101
Methodist Church, 97
Middleton, Catherine, 60, *60*
military, 46, *46*, 49, 54, *54*
mills, 52
mining, 35, 72, 73, 77–78
monarchs
    Anglo-Saxons, 93
    Arthur, 40, *40*
    Athelstan, 41

Charles I, 46
Elizabeth I, 45
Elizabeth II, 47, *58*, 60, 74, *74*, 133
Ethelbert, 94
George I, 47
George III, 49
Harold II, 41
Henry II, 95
Henry V, 84–85, 106
Henry VI, 43
Henry VII, 44, 45
Henry VIII, 44, 45, *45*, 96, 101, 133
James I, 45, 98, 125
James II, 47
John, 43, *43*
Mary, 47
modern role of, 59
Richard II, 43–44
Richard III, 44, 106
succession of, 42–43, 60–61
Victoria, 49
William III, 47
William the Conqueror, 41, 42, 77
moors, 15, 22, *22*, 31, 32
music, 68, *92*, *100*, 101–103, *102*, *103*, 133
mythical creatures, 60, 84, 94, *94*

N
national anthem, 68
National Archives, *42*
national bird, 31
national flag, 60, *60*
National Gallery, 76
national holidays, 125–127
national parks, 17, 25, 33, *33*
National Trails, 27, 33
natural gas, 78
Needles, 20
Nesbit, Edith, 104
New Forest, 29, 30
Newfoundland, 44
Newquay, 18, *18*
Newton, Isaac, 111–112, 133
New Zealand, 48
Norfolk Broads. *See* Fen Country.
Norfolk County, 33, 38
Norman Conquest, 41–42, 99

Norman people, 41–42, 83
Norsemen. *See* Vikings.
North East region, 13
Northern Ireland, 10, 45, 54, 61, 67
North Riding County, 13
North Sea, 17, 78
Northumberland National Park, 33
North West region, 13, 24, 29
Notting Hill Carnival, *126, 127*
nuclear power, 78

O
Oasis (musical group), 103
oil industry, 72, 73
Oliver, Jamie, 117
Olympic Games, 57, *57, 111*
Orwell, George, 105
otters, *29*
Oxford University, 121

P
Pakistan, 56, 86, 88, 89, *89*, 90, 98, 118
Parliament, 45, 46, 47, 59, 61–63, *63*,
    64, 65, 67, 69, 125
Peak District, 23, 25, 33
Peak District National Park, 25, 33
peers of the realm, 62
Pennine Mountains, 15, 33
people
    Angles, 36, 39, 93, 94
    Anglo-Saxons, 40, 93–94
    Beaker People, 35
    Celts, 36, 37, 38, 93
    children, *82, 84, 92, 116*, 120, *120,*
        122, 122
    clans, 36
    clothing, *84*, 125, *125*
    Druids, 93
    early settlers, 35
    education, 64, *116*, 119–121, *120,*
        121, 123, *123*
    foods, 71, 72, 74, *74*, 117–119, *118,*
        119
    games, 122, *122*
    housing, *55, 57, 61*, 124–125, *124*
    Iceni, 38, *39*
    immigration, 56, *56*, 86, *86*, 88–91,
        88, 89, 118

jobs, 20, 56, 57, 73, 75
Jutes, 39
land ownership, 41–42
languages, 36, 39, 40, 66, 83–85, *84,*
    86–87, 98
Normans, 41–42, 83
plague, 44, *44*
population, *18*, 25, 66, 86, 87, *87,*
    88, 91
Saxons, 36, 39, 40, 41, 93, 94
slavery, 37, 48
Vikings, 40–41, 83
plague, 44, *44*
plant life
    forests, 32
    heaths, 32
    hedgerows, 31
    Major Oak, 32, *32*
    Sites of Special Scientific Interest
        (SSSIs), 33
    wildflowers, 32
Poland, 88, *88*, 89
pollution, 77
ponies, 29–30, *30*
Poole, 19, 77
population, *18*, 25, 66, 86, 87, *87*, 88, 91
Port of London, 74
Portsmouth, 24
Potter, Beatrix, 104, *104*
pound sterling (currency), 56, 74, *74*
prehistoric life, 20, *20*, 27–28, 36
Presbyterianism, 97
prime ministers, 59, 63–64, *63, 64*, 69
Protestantism, 47, 96, 125
Punjabi language, 86
Puritans, 46

Q
Queen Elizabeth Olympic Park, 57
queens. *See* monarchs.

R
Radcliffe, Daniel, 108
railroads, 53, *53*, 75, 80–81, *80, 81*
Ramadan, 127
recipe, 118
red deer, 28–29, *28*
red grouse, 31

regions, 13, *13*
religion
    Alban (saint), 93–94
    Anglican Church, 96, 97
    Anglo-Saxons, 93–94
    Archbishops of Canterbury, 94, 95,
        96, *96*
    Bible, 98, *98*
    British Social Attitudes survey, 97
    Buddhism, 99
    Church of England, 44, 46, 62, 96
    Danelaw, 40
    Druidry, 93
    George, patron saint of England, 60
    Hinduism, 99, *99*
    holidays, 127
    Islamic, 57, 98, 99, 127
    Judaism, 99
    Methodist Church, 97
    monasteries, 40
    mosques, 98
    pilgrims, 95, *95*
    Presbyterianism, 97
    Protestantism, 47, 96, 125
    Puritans, 46
    Roman Catholic Church, 44, 46, 47,
        61, 83, 96, 97, *97*, 125
    Salisbury Cathedral, *92*
    Sikhism, 99
    Stonehenge, 35, 36, *36*, 76, 93
    Westminster Cathedral, 97
renewable energy, 78–79, *78*
Richard II, king of England, 43–44
Richard III, king of England, 44, 106
River Derwent, 52
River Thames, 16, 19, *19, 35*, 77, 81
roadways, *50*, 79, *79*
Rolling Stones (musical group), 102
Rolls-Royce company, 73, *73*
Roman Catholic Church, 44, 46, 47,
    61, 83, 96, 97, *97*, 125
Roman Empire, 36–39, *37*, 66, 83, 93
Romeo and Juliet (William Shakespeare),
    106, *106*
Rowling, J. K., 104, 105, *105*, 133, *133*
Royal Academy of Dramatic Art, 107
rugby, 115

Rushdie, Salman, 90–91
Rutland County, 13

S

sailing, 115, *115*
Salisbury Cathedral, *92*
Salisbury Plain, 36
Saxon people, 36, 39, 40, 41, 93, 94
Scafell Pike, 15, 16
Scotland, 9, 10, 15, 37, 45, 51, 60, 61, 67
service industries, 20, 73–76
Severn River, 19
Sewell, Anna, 104
Shah Jahan Mosque, 98
Shakespeare, William, 13, 106, 133
Shard London Bridge, 66, 67
Sheffield, 25, *25*, 86
Shelley, Percy Bysshe, 31
shipping industry, 53, 75
Sikhism, 99
Sites of Special Scientific Interest (SSSIs), 33
skylarks, 31–32
slavery, 37, 48
soccer. *See* football.
social housing, 124
Somerset County, 38
South Downs National Park, 33
South East region, 13, 18, 32
South West Coast Path, *26*, 27
South West region, 13, 18
Spanish Armada, 45, 48
sports, 57, 90, 113–115, *114*, *116*
Staffordshire County, 23
steam engine, 51, *51*, 53
steel industry, 25, 72
Stephenson, George, 53
St. George's Cross (national flag), 60, *60*
Stockton and Darlington Railway, *53*
Stonehenge, 35, 36, *36*, 76, 93
subway systems, 81, *81*
Suffolk County, 28
Supreme Court, 65, 67, 68
Sussex County, 18
swans, 31

T

Tate Britain museum, 110
Tate Modern museum, 76, 110
tea, 118, *119*
television, 106–107, 108–109, *108*, *109*, 117
tennis, 115
terrorism, 57
textile industry, 52, *52*, *72*
Thames Estuary, 81
Thanet Offshore Wind Farm, 78, *78*
thatched cottages, 124, *124*
Thatcher, Margaret, 64, *64*
Tolkien, J. R. R., 105
tourism, 20, 76, *76*, 77
Tower Hamlets borough, 90, 98
towns. *See also* cities; villages.
    Bath, 38, *38*
    Glastonbury, *124*
    Newquay, 18, *18*
    Poole, 19, 77
trade, 35, 38, 48, 64
transportation, 25, 53, *53*, 67, 75, 79–81, *79*, *80*, *81*
Transport for London system, 81
Trevithick, Richard, 53
Troyes, Chrétien de, 40
Turner, J. M. W., 110, *110*
Twenty20 cricket, 115

U

Uffington White Horse, 21, *21*
Union Jack (flag), 60
United Kingdom, 10, 11, 45, 54, 59, 60, 61, 78, 87, 121
United States, 12, 13, 25, 49, 54, 55, 68, 74, 77, 79, 83, 85, 88, 109
University of Cambridge, 121, *121*
University of East London, 75

V

Victorian Era, 49
Victoria, queen of England, 49
Vikings, 40–41, 83
villages. *See also* cities; towns.
    Cotswolds, 33, *33*
    Flash, 23
    houses in, 125

main streets, 125
Queen Elizabeth Olympic Park, 57

W

Wales, 9, 10, 15, 27, 44, 45, 61, 67
Wars of the Roses, 43
Warwick Castle, *76*, 77
Wash, 33
Watson, Emma, 108
Watt, James, 51, *51*, 53
Wells, H. G., 105
West Midlands region, 13, 25
Westminster Abbey, 60
Westminster Cathedral, 97
West Riding County, 13
West Saxon language, 84
White Cliffs of Dover, *17*, 19, 21, 33
wildflowers, 32
wildlife. *See* animal life; marine life; mythical creatures; plant life; prehistoric life.
William, duke of Cambridge, 60, *60*, 61
William III, king of England, 47
Williams, Rowan, Archbishop of Canterbury, 96
William the Conqueror, 41, 42, 77
Wimbledon tennis tournament, 115
Windermere (lake), 15, 16
wind farms, 78, *78*
Windsor Castle, 60
woolly mammoths, 28
World Cup football tournament, 113–114
World War I, 54, *54*
World War II, 55, *55*, 62, 91
Wren, Christopher, 47

Y

Yorkshire County, *12*, 13, 22, 25
Yorkshire and the Humber region, 13
Yorkshire pudding, 117
Young British Artists, 110–111

Meet the Author

A LOVER OF THE INTERNET, CHILDREN, ENGLAND, travel, books, cats, and just about everything else, the author Jean F. Blashfield delights in sharing what she enjoys with other people. Sometimes, she says, her biggest problem is figuring out what to leave out of a book because she is fascinated by every bit of information.

This was especially true for this book on England, because she's been there so often. She first visited England on a college choir tour. Enchanted by what she saw, she made up her mind to go back. After developing the *Young People's Science Encyclopedia* for Children's Press, she kept that promise to herself and returned to London to live. During her three years in London, she took every opportunity to travel, visiting the Lake District, Cornwall, and many places in between. She went to theaters, ballets, concerts, art galleries, and libraries, absorbing all she could of contemporary London. Since then, she has returned to England often. She is a regular reader of British publications because she likes to stay current with her friends who live in England. That habit gave her a head start on this book.

Blashfield has written more than 160 books, most of them for young people. Many of them have been for Scholastic's

Enchantment of the World and America the Beautiful series. She has also created an encyclopedia of aviation and space, written books on subjects ranging from murderers to house plants, and had a lot of fun creating a book on women's exploits called *Hellraisers, Heroines, and Holy Women.*

Born in Madison, Wisconsin, Blashfield grew up near Chicago, Illinois. She graduated from the University of Michigan and worked for publishers in Chicago and New York, and for NASA in Washington, D.C. She returned to Wisconsin when she married Wallace Black, a publisher, writer, and pilot, and began to raise a family. She has two grown children, one a professor of medieval history and one who manages a department at Stanford University, and three grandchildren.

Photo Credits